BIG
ENGLISH 4
PLUS

Mario Herrera • Christopher Sol Cruz

PUPIL'S BOOK

Contents

CLIL/Culture	Writing	Phonics	Values	I can...
Science: Twins, triplets and quadruplets exactly, fingerprint, fraternal, identical, look like, rare, relationship, survive **Around the World: Beards and moustaches** category, hairstyle, manly, prehistoric, shave	Parts of a Paragraph	**ear, air** dear, fear, hear, near, year chair, fair, hair, pair, stairs	Be considerate to others.	...make comparisons. ...describe people. ...talk about twins, triplets and quadruplets. ...write a paragraph.
Social Science: Advertising advertisement, attractive, billboard, bright, catch your eye, character, jingle, product, slogan, tool, tune **Around the World: Unusual habits** librarian, weird	Sequence Words	**ir, ur** bird, girl, sir, shirt, skirt curl, fur, hurt, surf, turn	Practise good habits.	...talk about what people do/are going to do and where they go at different times. ...say how often people do things. ...talk about adverts and how they work.
Science: Healthy eating balanced diet, dairy fat, grains, protein, salty, sugary, wholemeal **Around the World: School lunches** canteen, filling, lunch box, maize, organic, risotto, tuna	Conjunctions: *because* and *so*	**le, el, al, il** apple, bubble, uncle camel, towel, travel local, medal, sandals April, pencil, pupil	Choose healthy foods.	...talk about what people eat. ...make polite requests. ...talk about a balanced diet. ...find and use *because* and *so*.
Science: Germs bacteria, disease, enemy, fever, fungi, germ, malaria, microscope, protect, protozoa, spread, virus, vomit **Around the World: Home remedies** cure, ease, herbal, massage, painkiller, relax, stress, vinegar	Using Commas	**kn, wr** knee, knight, knock, knot, know wrap, wreck, wrist, write, wrong	Don't spread germs.	...talk about illnesses and health problems. ...ask for and give advice and make suggestions. ...talk about different kinds of germs. ...use commas correctly.
Science: Endangered animals cave, endangered, fur, in the wild, pond, predator, protect, trap **Around the World: Dragons** evil, extinction, magical, mythical	End Marks	**ph, wh** dolphin, elephant, phantom, phone, photo whale, wheat, wheel, when, white	Protect endangered animals.	...talk about animals and why some are endangered. ...ask questions and talk about abilities. ...use end marks correctly.
Maths: Multiplication average speed, distance travelled, multiply, number of, per hour **Around the World: Traditional cultures** dialect, herd, basic necessities, nomadic, running water, tundra	Speech Marks	**ge, dge** age, cage, large, page, sponge badge, bridge, edge, fridge, hedge	Solve problems.	...talk about the past and the present. ...talk about what people used to do. ...calculate average speed. ...use speech marks correctly.
Geography: World festivals attraction, celebrate, feast, fight, glacier, powder, take place, torch, unusual **Around the World: Leap years** propose marriage, superstition	Emails	**ue, u_e, ure** blue, glue, true cube, cute, duke, huge nature, picture, treasure	Celebrate traditions.	...talk about special days and dates. ...talk about the past and the future. ...talk about world festivals. ...write an email.
History: Hobbies from the past creativity, croquet, embroidery, employers, handmade, imagination, insect, needle, net, sewing, spare time, thread **Around the World: Unusual museums** coral, dust, lock of hair, marine life, potter	Informal Letters	**y, igh** by, fly, my, sky, try fight, high, light, night, right	Be a good sport.	...talk about people's hobbies. ...make comparisons. ...talk about hobbies in the past. ...write an informal letter.
Science: Body movement bone, brain, contract, flexible, joint, motion, muscle, nerves, organs, precision, relax, skeleton, support **Around the World: Extraordinary kids** effort, legend, professional, talent	Reviews	**ew, ey, e_e** dew, few, new, stew grey, hey, prey, they eve, gene, these	Learn new things.	...talk about things people know how to do. ...give opinions and make offers and quick decisions. ...describe how my body moves. ...write a review.

Unit 1 Kids in My Class

1 Listen, look and say.

Class Yearbook

Sylvia has got brown hair. She carries a **bright** pink backpack.

Natalie has got **wavy blonde** hair. She's **clever** and likes to read.

Trish is **tall** and has got **long light** brown hair. She plays the flute.

Darren is **short**. He has got **straight** black hair and glasses. He's **shy**.

Brian has got **dark** brown hair and **glasses**. He's **serious**.

Larry has got **light** brown hair. He's **friendly** and very **funny**.

2 Listen, find and say.

3 Play a game.

4 Listen, look and sing. Which girl is Marie?

Who's That Girl?

It's the first day of school.
We're back in our classes.
Everybody looks different
And I've got new glasses!

Who's that girl
Standing over there?
She's taller than me.
She's got curly dark hair.

**In my class are the same friends I know.
But we all change. We all grow. (x2)**

It's the first day of school
And I'm back in my chair.
Everybody looks different.
Now I've got straight hair.

Who's that girl?
Oh, wait, that's Marie!
Last time I saw her,
She was shorter than me!

Chorus

5 Look at the people in 1 and say True or False.

1 Sylvia has got brown hair. 2 Natalie wears glasses. 3 Larry is shy.

4 Brian is serious. 5 Trish plays the saxophone. 6 Darren is tall.

6 Ask and answer about people in your class.

She's tall and has got long black hair. Who is she?

It's Sarah.

THINK BIG Do people in the same family always look the same?
Do they sometimes look different?

Story

7 **Listen and read. Who's taller? Amanda or Christina?**

1 Christina tells her dad about the new girl at school.

2 Christina and the new girl have got some things in common.

3 But Christina and Amanda are different in some ways, too.

4 Amanda is shorter than Christina.

5   Christina likes her new classmate.

6   Christina is definitely not shy!

8   **Copy the chart. Then read and ✔ or ✘.**

	Christina...	Amanda...
1 has got curly dark hair.		
2 has got long hair.		
3 is tall.		
4 is nice and clever.		
5 is shy.		

THINK BIG   **Think of a friend. Explain how you are the same and how you are different.**

8

9 Listen and look at the sentences. Help Sam and Christina make more.

shorter darker longer smaller brighter

Chris is taller than Tom .

Kevin's hair is shorter than John's .

Mary's backpack is heavier than Kim's .

10 Copy the chart. Then complete.

+er		y +ier		double consonant + er	
¹🔑	straighter	curly	³🔑	⁵🔑	bigger
light	²🔑	⁴🔑	wavier	red	⁶🔑

11 Look at the picture. Make sentences using **than**.

heavy light long short tall

Mia

Juan

1 Juan is 🔑 Mia.

2 Mia is 🔑 Juan.

3 Mia's hair is 🔑 Juan's.

4 Juan's hair is 🔑 Mia's.

5 Juan's backpack is 🔑 Mia's.

12 **Read. Then complete the sentences.**

I	my	mine	she	her	hers
you	your	yours	we	our	ours
he	his	his	they	their	theirs

My sister's hair is longer than my hair.　My sister's hair is longer than mine.
My brother's hair is curlier than your hair.　My brother's hair is curlier than ¹❓.
My hair is straighter than his hair.　My hair is straighter than ²❓.
Our class is bigger than their class.　Our class is bigger than ³❓.

13 **Make new sentences.**

> hers　mine　ours　yours

1 My sister is younger than **your sister**.

2 His book is heavier than **her book**.

3 Leyla's hair is shorter than **my hair**.

4 Their car is bigger than **our car**.

14 **Make sentences.**

1 my sister/tall/yours
2 his backpack/heavy/mine
3 Leyla's legs/long/his
4 my eyes/dark/hers
5 their house/small/ours

15 **Describe things in your class with a partner.**

 Lisa's glasses are darker than Kim's.

Hakan's backpack is brighter than John's.

16 **Look at the people in your class. What's the same? Find and make sentences. Are there any twins?**

> eye colour   hair   hair colour   height   nose

> Paulo and Juan have got the same hair!

17 **Listen and read. What are two types of twin?**

> **CONTENT WORDS**
> exactly   fingerprint   fraternal   identical
> look alike   rare   relationship   survive

Twins and More!

1   Are your brothers and sisters older than you or younger than you? Sometimes brothers and sisters are exactly the same age. This happens when a mother has more than one baby at the same time. If there are two babies at the same time, we call them twins. Triplets means three babies and quadruplets means four babies!

2   One out of every 32 births is a pair of twins. One birth in every 625 is triplets, and quadruplets (four babies) and larger groups are quite rare. Only 1 in every 9,000 births is quadruplets. This is because it's more difficult for quadruplet babies to survive.

3   Do twins always look the same? The answer is no. There are two types of twin. Identical twins look exactly alike but other twins are called fraternal: they don't look alike. Fraternal twins are much more common than identical twins: only 30% of all twins are identical and 70% are fraternal. In larger birth groups, identical babies are very rare. For example, only 8% of triplets are identical and 92% are fraternal. And there is only a 1% chance of identical quadruplets, so more than 99% of them are fraternal.

4   So are identical babies completely identical? Again, the answer is no. The hair, eyes, character and even foot size for identical babies can be the same. However, they've got different fingerprints. Also, sometimes twins can be like a mirror, for example when one twin is left-handed and the other twin is right-handed.

5   In 2010, researchers in Padova, Italy, showed images of twins growing inside their mother. These images tell us that twins really do have a special relationship. The twins touched each other more than they touched themselves. These little brothers and sisters begin to love each other even before they are born.

18 Copy the chart. Read quickly and complete.

Number of babies	Name	Number of births	% identical	% Fraternal
2	¹ 🔲	1 out of 32	² 🔲	70%
3	³ 🔲	⁴ 🔲	8%	⁵ 🔲
⁶ 🔲	quadruplets	1 out of 9,000	Less than 1%	⁷ 🔲

19 Look at **17** and say **True** or **False**. Correct the sentences that are false.

1 Twins, triplets and quadruplets are the same age.

2 There are more quadruplets than triplets.

3 Identical twins are more common than fraternal twins.

4 Identical twins aren't always exactly the same.

5 Identical twins have got the same fingerprints.

6 Twins growing inside their mothers often touch each other.

THINK BIG What are some good and bad things about having an identical twin?

PROJECT

20 Do a class survey about brothers and sisters. Ask and answer to complete the chart.

Number of brothers or sisters	Number of pupils	% of all pupils in class
none (only child)		
one		
two		
three		
four or more		
twins, triplets or quadruplets		

21 Look at **20**. What is more common in your class? What is less common? Make three sentences.

One brother or sister is more common than three brothers or sisters.

Grammar

22 **Listen and read. Which T-shirt does Ryan decide to buy?**

Ryan and Jenny are shopping.

Ryan: I can't decide which T-shirt to buy. This blue one's OK but is the white one nicer?

Jenny: I think the blue T-shirt is more interesting than the white one. Look, the fabric is better, too.

Ryan: Yes, you're right.

Jenny: And it's your colour. You look more handsome in it!

Ryan: Yes, it's perfect! Let's see how much it is… Oh! Um… I think I'll get the white one.

Jenny: But why?

Ryan: Because the blue T-shirt is also more expensive!

23 **Look at 22. Complete the charts.**

interesting	The blue T-shirt is ¹❓ **than** the white one.
handsome	You look ²❓ in the blue T-shirt.
expensive	The blue T-shirt is ³❓ **than** the white T-shirt.

But…	
good	The fabric is ⁴❓ .
bad	These jeans are **worse than** those jeans.

24 **Look at 23. Compare using the words in brackets.**

1 Adrianna is ❓ her sister. (beautiful)

2 Good idea! I think you're ❓ I am! (intelligent)

3 My friend Harry is ❓ everyone else in the class. (popular)

4 Selda's Maths grade is ❓ mine. (good)

5 Triplets are ❓ quadruplets. (common)

6 This place is awful! Their pizza is ❓ their burgers! (bad)

25 **Look and read. Then make sentences.**

Motorbike:
€400
Safety:
☆☆☆
Comfort:
☆☆

Car:
€30,000
Safety:
☆☆☆☆☆☆
Comfort:
☆☆☆☆☆

1 **cheap:**   The motorbike is ❓ the car.

2 **expensive:**   The car is ❓ the motorbike.

3 **safe:**   The car is ❓ the motorbike.

4 **dangerous:**   The motorbike is ❓ the car.

5 **comfortable:**   The car is ❓ the motorbike.

6 **uncomfortable:** The motorbike is ❓ the car.

26 **Look at 25. Make new sentences.**

27 **Read, ask and answer.**

1 difficult – Maths or History?

2 interesting – board games or computer games?

3 a good pet – a cat or a dog?

4 healthy – a good breakfast or a good dinner?

5 exciting – books or films?

6 funny – cartoons or comics?

Which is more difficult: Maths or Science?

I think Maths is more difficult than Science.

I don't agree. I think Science is more difficult than Maths!

28 **Look at 27. What do you think? In your notebook, write six sentences.**

Beards and Moustaches

1 This issue of *Fun Facts* looks at beards and moustaches and a very strange competition. How many of these things did you know?

> **FACT** Many Europeans believe a beard is very manly but in Asia and South America, beards are less popular.

> **FACT** Scientists believe prehistoric men had beards because a man with a beard is scarier than a man without a beard!

> **FACT** In ancient Greece, beards were very popular because Greeks thought men looked cleverer with a beard. But Alexander the Great changed this. Alexander was worried about enemies pulling his men's beards in battle, so all his men shaved!

2 Today, beard fashions still come and go. In 1990, a group of men in Germany didn't care about fashion but they loved strange beards and moustaches.

29 **Where are these hairstyles from? Look, guess and match. Then compare with the class.**

> England   France   Jamaica   Japan

a
b
c
d

30 **Which hairstyle do you like? Discuss with a partner.**

> I like picture b because I love colours.

> I like picture c more because...

31 **Read the article quickly. What's it about? Look and choose two.**
  a Beards in history
  b Women's hairstyles
  c An interesting competition
  d Life in Greece

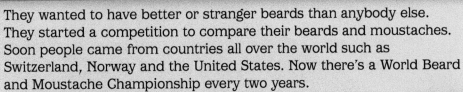

They wanted to have better or stranger beards than anybody else. They started a competition to compare their beards and moustaches. Soon people came from countries all over the world such as Switzerland, Norway and the United States. Now there's a World Beard and Moustache Championship every two years.

3   There are sixteen different categories of beards and moustaches at the Championship. The English Moustache is long and goes out to the sides. The Dalí Moustache is named after the famous Spanish painter Salvador Dalí. It's long and points straight up. The Verdi category gets its name from Italian composer Giuseppe Verdi. This style has a straight beard and a curly moustache. The Freestyle Beard is even funnier and more interesting! Competitors in this category don't have to follow specific rules. Their beards and moustaches can be any shape or style they like!

4   The competition takes place in a different country each time. In the World Beard and Moustache Championship, culture doesn't matter but the hair on your face does!

32 **Listen and read. Then choose the correct answer.**

1 Beards are more popular in...
   a Europe.   **b** South America.

2 Alexander the Great didn't like beards...
   a because people looked cleverer with them.   **b** because they were a problem in battles.

3 Who started the World Beard and Moustache Championship?
   a A group of Germans.   **b** Some men from Norway and Switzerland.

4 The beards and moustaches at the Championships...
   a have famous names.   **b** all copy the same style.

5 The Championships...
   a are in a different country each time.   **b** are always in Germany.

33 **Search for pictures of interesting hairstyles. Which styles do you like and why? Discuss with a classmate.**

THINK **BIG** **Has anyone in your family got a beard or a moustache? Do you like it? Why/Why not?**

Read. Then find the title, topic sentence, detail sentences and final sentence.

A title says what you are going to read about.

A topic sentence gives the main idea of a paragraph.

Detail sentences give us more information.

A final sentence talks about the subject in a different way.

My Best Friend

My best friend's name is Anita.

She's taller than me and her hair is longer than mine. Anita is clever and she's funny, too. We like playing computer games at the weekend.

I'm happy to have a friend like Anita.

Read the sentences and say title, topic sentence, detail sentence or final sentence.

1   She is very nice and a lot of fun.
2   I'm always happy to see Aunt Elsie.
3   She likes making biscuits with my sister and me.
4   My favourite aunt is Aunt Elsie.
5   My Aunt Elsie
6   She also likes playing games with us.

 **Look at 35. Order the sentences to make a paragraph.**

Writing Steps

 Write about a friend or relative.

1   Think of a friend or relative.
2   Make a list of what they are like and why you like him/her.
3   Write a title.
4   Write a topic sentence.
5   Write three detail sentences.
6   Write a final sentence.

15
38 **Listen, read and repeat.**

1 ear   **2** air

16
39 **Listen and find. Then say.**

hear

chair

17
40 **Listen and blend the sounds.**

1	f-ear	fear	**2**	y-ear	year
3	h-air	hair	**4**	p-air	pair
5	f-air	fair	**6**	d-ear	dear
7	n-ear	near	**8**	s-t-air-s	stairs

18
41 **Read aloud. Then listen and chant.**

A boy with big ears and fair hair,
Hears the twins on the stairs.
A boy with big ears and fair hair,
Hears the twins sit on their chairs.

42 **Listen and complete the sentences.**

dropped   first   help   turn

1 You can have a ❓.

2 Can I ❓ you?

3 You can go ❓.

4 You ❓ something.

 Practise being considerate with a partner.

 You can go first.

Thank you!

PROJECT

 Make Good Manners award ribbons. Your teacher can give them to pupils who are considerate and have got good manners.

Good Manners

Complete the dialogue.

better   blonde   clever   darker   different
he   more   serious   taller   yours

A: Is that your brother?

B: Yes, that's Max. We're not the same, we're very ¹? . He's more ²? than I am. He's quite shy.

A: Are you ³? playful than he is?

B: Absolutely! And I'm ⁴? than ⁵? is.

A: Yes, he's shorter and his hair is ⁶? than ⁷? .

B: Yes. I've got ⁸? hair. His is brown.

A: Is he ⁹? ?

B: Yes, he's very good at Maths. But I'm ¹⁰? at sport!

 Make cards with the words below. Then play a game.

big   bright   curly   dark   heavy   light   long   short   small   tall

Allie's hair is longer than mine.

long

I Can

- make comparisons.
- describe people.
- talk about twins, triplets and quadruplets.
- write a paragraph.

Unit 2 Our Schedule

1 Listen, look and say.

1 go to the dentist

2 go on holiday

3 go to a wedding

4 visit my grandparents

5 eat out

6 have a guitar lesson

2 Listen, find and say.

3 Play a game.

23 24

4 **Listen and sing. Find the nine activities Sam does.**

Things We Do!

There are lots and lots of things
That I do every day,
Like go to school, watch a film,
Stay up late and play!

But there are lots of other things
I don't want to do so much,
Like go to the dentist, do the dishes,
Make my bed and such.

How often do you do these things?
Every day? Once a week? Once a year?

I take out the rubbish
On Tuesdays before school.
And I feed our funny cat
But I don't mind — she's cool.

Chorus

25

5 **Listen and complete.**

1 I ❓ dentist twice a year. **2** They ❓ every winter.

3 She ❓ with her parents every Friday. **4** We ❓ four times a month.

6 **Look at 1. Ask and answer for you. Use the words from the box.**

once *   twice **   three times ***   every day/week/month/year/summer

How often do you
go to the dentist?

I go three
times a year.

THINK BIG **What activities should you do once a day? Explain.**

7 **Listen and read. Where is Christina going this weekend?**

A Lot of Weddings!

What are you doing this weekend, Amanda?

I'm going to my grandma's house.

1 Christina and Amanda are talking about their weekend plans.

How often do you see your grandma?

Monday
Tuesday
Wednesday
Thursday
Friday
Saturday
Sunday

Every Saturday.

2 Amanda sees her grandma once a week.

How about you? What are you doing this weekend?

I'm going to my cousin's wedding.

3 Christina isn't happy about her weekend plans.

Oh! Do you like going to weddings?

No, I don't because I have to wear a dress.

4 Christina doesn't like wearing dresses.

Panel 5:
How often do you go to weddings?

About three times a year. I've got lots of cousins!

5 Christina has to go to a lot of weddings.

Panel 6:
Wow! That's a lot of weddings!

And a lot of dresses for me!

6 Christina is thinking about all the dresses she has to wear to her cousins' weddings.

8 Find the mistakes and correct the sentences.

1 Amanda is going to her friend's house this weekend.
2 Amanda visits her grandma every Sunday.
3 Christina is going to her uncle's wedding.
4 Christina is happy about her weekend.
5 Christina goes to weddings three times a week.
6 Christina likes wearing dresses.

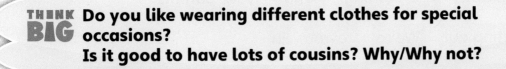

THINK BIG Do you like wearing different clothes for special occasions?
Is it good to have lots of cousins? Why/Why not?

28

9 Listen and look at the sentences. Help Sam and Christina make more.

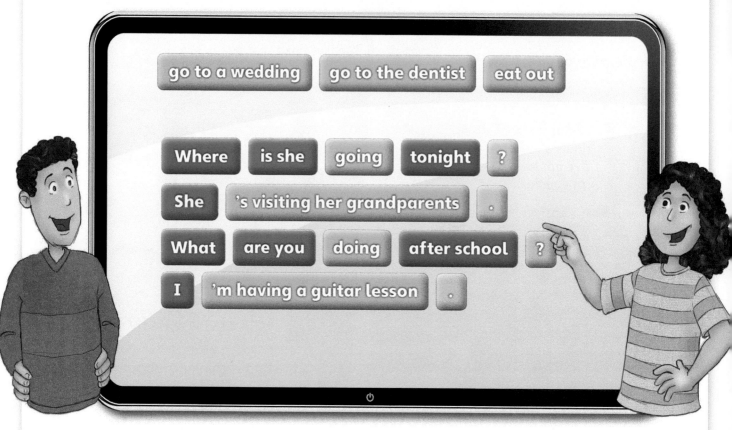

go to a wedding   go to the dentist   eat out

Where | is she | going | tonight | ?

She | 's visiting her grandparents | .

What | are you | doing | after school | ?

I | 'm having a guitar lesson | .

10 Complete the questions. Then match.

1 ❓ are they doing after school?   **a** She's going to the library.

2 ❓ is your sister going?   **b** They're going shopping.

3 ❓ are we going after dinner?   **c** He's helping in the school garden.

4 ❓ is Mr Lee doing after school?   **d** We're visiting our grandparents.

11 Put the words in order. Make questions and answers. Then make your own to test your partner.

1 he   tomorrow?   Where   is   going

2 tonight?   are   doing   What   your parents

3 eating out   We're   town.   in

4 going   are   on   My family   holiday   this summer.

5 visiting   He's   his   next   weekend.   friend

12 **Read. Then put the phrases in the word box in order. Start with twice a day. Then make sentences for you.**

> twice a week ▶ every Thursday ▶ once a month ▶ three times a year ▶ every summer

> every month   every spring   every Tuesday
> once a day   three times a week   twice a day
> twice a year

I visit my grandparents every month.

What do you do every month?

13 **Answer the questions for you.**

1 How often do you go to the dentist?
2 How often do you play sports?
3 How often does your English teacher give tests?
4 How often does your best friend come to your house?

14 **Correct these sentences for you.**

1 I go to the dentist once a week.
2 My family eat out every weekend.
3 My sister does the dishes twice a year.
4 My grandma makes her bed every winter.
5 I go to a wedding every Saturday.

15 **Ask and answer.**

What are you doing this weekend?

I'm going to the park and eating out on Sunday.

How often do you eat out?

About once a month.

16 Read the sentences. Which sentences are true for you? Then ask and answer about your classmates.

1 I like watching adverts on TV.

2 Information in adverts is always true.

3 Adverts are important.

30

17 Listen and read. Which four tools do advertisers use?

CONTENT WORDS

advertisement   attractive   billboard   bright   catch your eye
character   jingle   product   slogan   tool   tune

Advertising

Buy it now!
Only €2.99

Adele's favourite cereal

Washes whiter and faster

For a healthy and happy life

1   Companies put advertisements everywhere. They're all around you – on TV and websites, in newspapers, in magazines and on the radio. They're even on billboards along the side of the road. Why are they there? That's simple! Companies want you to buy things and advertising makes you want to buy those things. How? Advertisements tell you that a product is going to make you happier or more popular. They even tell you the product is going to make you look more attractive, older or younger. Usually these messages aren't true. The company just wants your money!

2   When companies are making an advertisement, they think: "Who's going to buy this product? What do they like? What do they want to see or hear?" They use the answers to these questions to help them make the advertisement. There are four special tools that advertisers often use. Watch out for them!

3 **a**   A character or cartoon can help sell food. Advertisers put them on boxes of cereal or children's food. Children see the characters and they want to buy that cereal or food.

b   Famous people can also help sell a product. When a famous person uses a product, we want to use it, too. For example, famous sports people can sell trainers and famous actors can sell coffee, perfume or beauty products.

c   Slogans and jingles are a clever way to sell. These are words or tunes that you remember all day. In fact, you can't forget them! When you see a product, you think of that tune or slogan.

d   Bright colours and interesting images catch your eye and sell things, too.

4   Of course advertisements are fun but next time you see a really good advertisement, just ask yourself: "What's it trying to sell? Do I really want or need this product?" That way, you're deciding, not the advertiser.

18 **Look at 17. Read and match.**

1 Companies make advertisements
2 Advertisements tell you that
3 The messages in advertisements
4 Advertisers use
5 You can sell things to children
6 Jingles or slogans are a clever tool

a aren't usually true.
b using cartoon characters.
c because they want to sell things.
d you'll be happier if you buy something.
e because you can't forget them.
f four tools when making an advertisement.

19 **Copy the chart. Read and complete. Give examples from your country.**

Advertising tool	Why does it work?	Example from my country
Slogans and jingles	¹	
²	We want to use the same things	
³	⁴	
⁵	Children like the characters	

 THINK BIG **Where do adverts sell more things? Why?**
on TV   on websites   in magazines and newspapers   on the radio

PROJECT

20 **Make an advert. Then present it to the class.**

1 Choose and use advertising tools from the article.
2 Make your advertisement.
3 Put your advertisement on the wall. Which tools did your friends use?

FANTASTIC BIKE!

This fantastic bike makes you go faster.

Grammar

 21 **Listen and read. What's Jacob going to wear today?**

Jacob is talking to his mum. He's going to visit his friend.

Mum: Are you going to wear your jacket today, Jacob?

Jacob: No, I'm not, Mum. This shirt is fine. It's my favourite.

Mum: But the weather isn't going to be very good!

Jacob: It looks sunny now. Tom's mum is going to take us to the beach, remember?

Mum: Well, you're going to get wet if it rains.

Jacob: Oh, Mum. Of course I'm going to get wet. I'm going to go swimming in the sea!

22 **Look at 21. Complete the charts.**

✔	I	'm		
	He/She/It	¹☐	going ⁴☐	⁵☐ very good.
	We/You/They	²☐		⁶☐ us to the beach.
✘	I	'm not		⁷☐ wet.
	He/She/It	³☐		⁸☐ swimming.
	We/You/They	aren't		

Am	I		⁹☐ your jacket?	Yes, ... **am.** / No, ¹⁰☐.
Is	he/she/it	**going to**	visit my friend?	Yes, ... **is.** / No, ... **isn't.**
Are	we/you/they		be cold?	Yes, ... **are.** / No, ... **aren't.**

What **When**	**am** I		do?
	is he/she/it	**going to**	take?
	are we/you/they		wear?

23 **Choose the correct answer.**

1 It ❓ to be very hot at the weekend.
   a going   **b** 's going

2 Fatma's going ❓ a dress to the party.
   a wear   **b** to wear

3 They're ❓ the ten o'clock train.
   a catch   **b** going to catch

4 Francis and I ❓ visit Madrid.
   a aren't going to   **b** am not going to

5 Run, it's starting to rain! You're going ❓ .
   a to get wet   **b** to wet

24 **Look and say. Use he/she/it/they, going to and the words from the box.**

> have pizza tonight   not go to school   not rain today
> not watch the film   sing a song   wait a long time

1

2

3

4

5

6

25 **Sienna's family has a busy week. Look and read. Write questions and answers in your notebook. Use going to.**

Monday – Sienna – dentist 3 p.m.
Tuesday – Mum – go food shopping
Thursday – Aunty Violet – cook for the wedding
Friday – Harriet – go to hairdresser
Saturday – Harriet and James – THE BIG DAY
Sunday – Everybody – have a rest!

1 What/Sienna/do on Monday?

2 Who/go to the hairdresser?

3 When/Mum/go food shopping?

4 Mum/cook for the wedding?

5 What/James/do on Saturday?

http://www.unusualhabits.com

Unusual Habits

	Started by ABC_girl 11:28 a.m. reply	Hi, everyone! I'm eleven years old and I'm from London. I've got a question for you: am I crazy?!? I always put the books on my bookshelf in alphabetical order. If one is in the wrong place, I move it. I've got 200 books: that's a lot! I check them every week. My mum's a librarian and she says it's easy to find my books with this system. But is this weird? What do you think?
	racerXYZ 11:32 a.m. reply	This isn't weird, ABC_girl! Listen to this: I've got a strange habit, too. I never touch doorknobs. I really like sliding doors because they haven't got doorknobs. It's lucky that I live in Tokyo, Japan. There are lots of sliding doors here!

26 Ask and answer with a partner. Share with the class.

1 How often do you tidy your room?

2 Do you have a favourite toy or object? What is it?

3 Do you like eating or drinking strange things? What are they?

I love ketchup sandwiches. They're delicious!

I tidy my room every day after school. I like to be tidy and organised.

27 Read the web forum quickly. Which sentences are true? Choose two.

1 ABC_girl has got a strange habit.

2 Everyone thinks ABC_girl is crazy.

3 ABC_girl asks for people's opinions.

4 People write about ABC_girl's habit.

birdsong
11:38 a.m.
reply

Hey! Here's my strange habit: I have a shower three times a day! I know it's a lot but I live in Libya, Africa. It's REALLY hot and the showers cool me down. I also like to feel clean!

snowflake
11:43 a.m.
reply

My habit isn't that unusual because I live on a farm. I drink fresh milk twice a day. It's delicious! However, my glass of milk is always with ice. I can only drink REALLY cold milk. Weird!

hatman22
11:44 a.m.
reply

I wear a hat every day. I wear it to school. I wear it to bed. I even wear it in the shower! I imagine that's pretty unusual. But it's cold where I live – in Rio Grande, Argentina.

tbear02
11:57 a.m.
reply

I'm a bit like you, ABC_girl. I make my bed every morning, then I put all my toy animals on the bed. The animals have to be in the same place every day. I've got fifty toy animals of different shapes and sizes. It's weird but I'm not crazy.

33

28 Listen and read. Match the people to the facts.

1 ABC_girl　　**2** racerXYZ　　**3** birdsong　　**4** snowflake

a He/She lives near animals.
b He/She has got lots of things.
c He/She has got a habit because of the weather.
d He/She likes to be tidy.
e He/She likes drinking something cold.
f He/She can't touch something.

29 Choose a habit or use your idea. Answer and write in your notebook.

1 What's your habit?
2 Where are you from?
3 Is your habit unusual?
4 Is your habit strange in your country?

I eat chocolate three times a day.

I take my lucky toy everywhere.

I wash my hands twenty times a day.

I only drink one kind of juice.

THINK BIG Has anyone in your family got an unusual habit? What is it? Why is it unusual?

30 **Read and find.**

> Sequence words tell the order in which things happen. Here are some examples:
>
> **My Day at School**
>
> First, we've got a Maths lesson.
> Next, we've got a spelling test.
> Then we have lunch.
> After that, we've got an English lesson.
> Finally, we've got a P.E. lesson.
>
> Use first for the first activity. Use finally for the last activity. For the activities in between, you can use the sequence words in any order.

This weekend, I'm going to visit my grandparents. First, we're going to the park to fly kites. Next, we're going to the zoo to feed the animals. Then we're going home for lunch. After that, we're playing basketball outside. Finally, we're going to watch a film and eat pizza!

31 **Complete with sequence words.**

My family and I always go to the beach on Saturdays in the summer. ¹ 🔖 , we go swimming in the sea. ² 🔖 , we have a picnic under our big yellow umbrella. ³ 🔖 my mum and dad read magazines and my brothers and I go swimming again all afternoon. ⁴ 🔖 , we all get in the car to go home. ⁵ 🔖 , we stop for ice cream!

32 **Write a list of things you do on Saturdays. Then number them in the correct order.**

33 **In your notebook, write a paragraph about what you do on Saturdays. Use sequence words. Share your paragraph with the class.**

35
34 **Listen, read and repeat.**

1 ir   **2** ur

 36
35 **Listen and find. Then say.**

bird

surf

 37
36 **Listen and blend the sounds.**

1 g-ir-l   girl   **2** sh-ir-t   shirt
3 f-ur   fur   **4** h-ur-t   hurt
5 s-k-ir-t   skirt   **6** s-ir   sir
7 c-ur-l   curl   **8** t-ur-n   turn

 38
37 **Read aloud. Then listen and chant.**

Two girls with red curls,
Two cats with black fur,
Two boys with white shirts,
Are watching birds!

38 Listen and read. Choose the happy face for good habits or the sad face for bad habits.

1 I make my bed every day. ☺ ☹

2 I eat vegetables only once a week. ☺ ☹

3 I do my homework and watch films at the same time. ☺ ☹

4 I help do the dishes every day. ☺ ☹

39 Talk about your habits with a partner.

I exercise three times a week.

That's a good habit!

PROJECT

40 Work with your classmates to make a Good Habits mural. Hang it on a wall in your school.

GOOD HABITS

Exercise often.

Eat vegetables every day.

Do your homework every day.

41 Look and answer the questions.

1
What are they going to do this summer?

2
Where is he going to go after school?

3
What are you going to do this afternoon?

42 Read and choose.

1 How **often/many** do you visit your grandparents?

2 We see them **once/times** a week. We go **on/every** weekend.

3 That's nice. My grandma **always/twice** makes a big pie. It's delicious!

4 Cool. I only see my grandparents **three/three times** a year.

43 Play the Silly Sentences game.

I Can

- talk about what people do/are going to do and where they go at different times.
- say how often people do things.
- talk about adverts and how they work.

Unit 3

1 **Listen, look and say.**

FOOD FAVOURITES

SPECIALS

1 steamed buns

2 chicken curry

3 porridge

4 watermelon

5 cereal with milk

6 lamb meatballs

7 noodle soup

8 paella

9 toasted cheese sandwich

2 **Listen, find and say.**

3 **Play a game.**

4 **Listen and sing. Find the food.**

Would You Like Some?

"Would you like some noodle soup?
Tonight it tastes really nice!"
Sam says, "No, Dad, not right now
But thanks so much — thanks, anyhow."

Come on, Sam, please have a little taste!
Come on, Sam, don't make a funny face!

"How about a sweet steamed bun?
It's really yummy. Come on, try one!"
Sam says, "No, Dad, not right now
But thanks so much — thanks, anyhow."

"Would you like some chicken curry?"
"No thanks, Dad. I'm in a hurry!"
Sam says, "No, Dad, not right now
But thanks so much — thanks, anyhow."

Chorus

"Come on, Sam. Just one little bite!"
"Oh, really, Dad. Oh, all right!
Mmm. Hey, you're right. It's great!
Please put some more on my plate!"

5 **Listen and say the food from 1.**

1	2	3	4	5

Isabella Spain	**Mei Lin** China	**Oliver** Scotland	**Ela** Turkey	**Alan** United States

THINK BIG Which child's meals in 5 do you like? Which do you not like?
What do you like eating for breakfast and for lunch?

6 Listen and read. Does Christina like Sam's cake?

HomemadeLemonade

Oh! Lemonade and cake! Mmm!

Would you like to try some?

1 Sam makes some lemonade and cake.

Mmm. Yes, I would.

What would you like first?

I'd like some cake, please.

2 Christina would like some cake.

How is it?

Um! It's... OK.

3 Christina doesn't like the cake.

Would you like some lemonade?

Yes, I would. Thanks!

4 Christina would like some lemonade.

Ugh! Yuck! What's in this lemonade?

5 | Christina can't drink the lemonade. It's too sour.

Oh... lemons... water... ice... and... Oh, no! I forgot the sugar!

I think you forgot the sugar in the cake, too!

6 | Sam realises why Christina doesn't like the lemonade and the cake.

7 Read and choose. Make correct sentences.

1 Sam makes some **lemons/lemonade** and cake.

2 Christina **wants/doesn't want** to try some.

3 First, she has **some cake/a lemon** but she doesn't like it.

4 Then she has some lemonade but she **can/can't** drink it.

5 In the lemonade, there's **oranges/lemons**, water and ice.

6 Sam forgot to put in the **salt/sugar**.

THINK BIG **Lemons are sour. Can you think of any other sour foods? Lemonade is sweet. Can you think of any other sweet foods? Which do you prefer? Sour food or sweet food?**

8 Listen and look at the sentences. Help Sam and Christina make more.

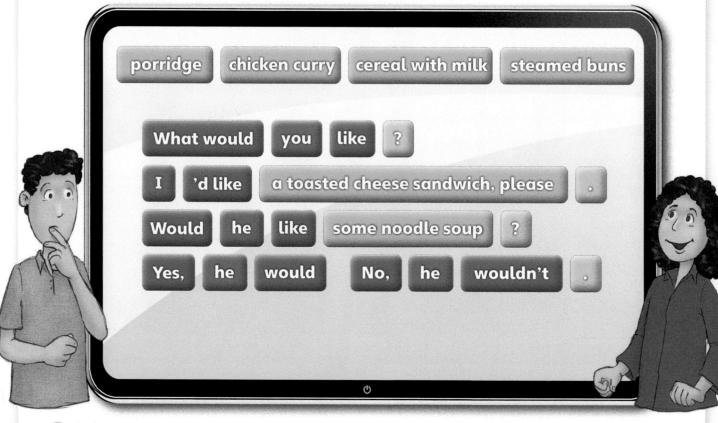

porridge   chicken curry   cereal with milk   steamed buns

What would | you | like | ?

I | 'd like | a toasted cheese sandwich, please | .

Would | he | like | some noodle soup | ?

Yes, | he | would | No, | he | wouldn't | .

9 Look and complete.

1 What ? Jessie ? ?
? some porridge.

2 What ? Jin-Soo ? ?
? some noodle soup.

3 What ? Ms Roberts ? ?
? some watermelon.

4 What ? you ? ?
?

10 **Copy the charts. Then complete with the correct form of** do, like **or** would like.

Do	you/we/they	¹🐾	curry?	Yes,	I/we/they	²🐾.	No,	I/we/they	³🐾.
Does	he/she	⁴🐾			he/she	⁵🐾.		he/she	⁶🐾.

⁷🐾	you	⁸🐾	to try some curry?	Yes,	I / he/she / we / they	⁹🐾.	No,	I / he/she / we / they	¹⁰🐾.
	he/she								
	they								

11 **Read and complete.**

1 Would your dad like to try a steamed bun? Yes, 🐾 .

2 Would your mum like to try some curry? No, 🐾 .

3 Would you and your friends like to try some lemonade? Yes, 🐾 .

4 Would you like to try some watermelon? 🐾

5 🐾 ? Yes, I would.

12 **Put the words in order to make answers. Then match.**

1 What would Helena like for breakfast?

2 What would you like for lunch?

3 What would your uncle like to try?

4 What would they like to eat?

5 Would they like a burger and chips?

6 Would you like to try some paella?

a some cake. to try like He'd

b apple. She'd like an

c would. Yes, I Thanks.

d please. I'd like noodle soup, some

e meatballs. They'd like lamb

f wouldn't. they No,

13 Ask and answer with a partner. How many people in your class have a healthy diet?

1 What's your favourite snack?

2 Do you eat vegetables with every meal?

3 How often do you eat meat?

4 Is your diet healthy?

50

 14 Listen and read. What does the plate show?

> **CONTENT WORDS**
> balanced diet   dairy   fat   grains   protein   salty   sugary   wholemeal

A Healthy Diet

1   It's breakfast time. You're hungry and you say, "Mum, can I have a chocolate muffin?" But your mum says, "How about something healthy? Shall we have cereal or some fruit for breakfast instead?" Why does your mum say this? Because your diet is important and a balanced diet is the best way to stay healthy. You should eat the right amount of grains, vegetables, fruit, protein (such as chicken) and dairy every day.

2   The chart below is called 'My Plate'. It shows the right balance of different food groups that your diet should contain. The Vegetables section is bigger than the Protein section, so you should eat more vegetables than protein. The Grains section is bigger than the Fruit section, so eat more grains (such as corn) than fruit. The Dairy section is smaller than the others, so eat fewer dairy foods (such as cheese and yoghurt) than any other.

My Plate

3   For a healthy body and mind, use the My Plate chart as a guide when you eat and follow these simple rules:

- Eat food you like but don't eat too much.
- Eat lots of fruit and vegetables – about half of what you eat should be fruit and vegetables such as apples, carrots and greens.
- Eat whole grains – half of your grains should be whole grains such as wholemeal bread and pasta.
- Choose fat-free or low-fat milk, rather than full-fat, as too much fat is bad for you.
- Stay away from food that's too salty.
- Drink lots of water and avoid sugary drinks.

4   Can you sometimes eat "bad" foods? Yes, you can, but don't eat them too often. If you fill half of your plate with vegetables and stay away from too much fat, sugar and salt, you'll stay in good health.

15 **Look at 14. Copy the chart and complete.**

Food group	Examples	Recommendations
Fruit and vegetables	¹ ?	Eat lots of these
² ?	³ ?	Choose fat-free or low-fat milk
Grains	Bread, pasta	⁴ ?
Protein	⁵ ?	Eat more vegetables than protein

16 **Look at 14 and say True or False. Correct the sentences that are false.**

1 A balanced diet is important for your health.

2 Eat more protein than vegetables.

3 Don't eat food you like.

4 Choose full-fat milk, as fat is good for you.

5 Don't eat too much dairy.

6 Eat more grains than fruit.

7 Fill half of your plate with sugar and salt.

THINK BIG What can happen when you don't eat a healthy diet?

PROJECT

17 **Create a Healthy Meal poster. Then present it to the class.**

Salad has got lots of vegetables in it.

This has grains and protein.

Low-fat yoghurt is better.

18 **Listen and read. Who wants to eat healthy food?**

Dan and his mum are shopping.

Mum: Come on, Dan. Let's get some lunch, I'm really hungry. Shall we buy some food here? How about trying that nice salad? It looks really healthy. Or how about that bean soup? That looks really good.

Dan: Oh, no, Mum. Can I sit down? I don't feel very well.

Mum: Yes, of course. Shall I get you some water?

Dan: No, thanks. Um, Mum? Can you buy me a cola instead, please? And can I have a burger, too? Look! Let's go to that place over there.

Mum: Oh, Dan!

19 **Look at 18. Complete the charts.**

¹🔲 I sit down? ²🔲 you ³🔲 me a cola, please? **Can** he/she/it/we/they come?	Yes, I/you/he/she/it/we/they **can**. Yes, ⁴🔲 course.
	No, I/you/he/she/it/we/they **can't**. Sorry, no.

⁵🔲 we buy some food here?	Yes, **let's**. / No, **let's not**.
⁶🔲 I ⁷🔲 you some water?	Yes, please. / No, ⁸🔲 .
⁹🔲 that bean soup? ¹⁰🔲 about ¹¹🔲 that nice salad? ¹²🔲 get some lunch. **Let's** ¹³🔲 to that place over there.	OK. That's a good idea. No, thanks.

20 **Look at 19. Read and choose.**

1 **How about/Shall we** buy some new clothes?
2 **Let's/Shall** have paella for dinner.
3 How about **watch/watching** a film tonight?
4 **Let's/Can** we have our dinner now.
5 Can we **have/having** a birthday party?

21 Look at 19. Read and choose.

1 **A:** Can I have some more rice?

    B: Yes, **let's/of course**. Give me your plate.

2 **A:** Can you help me, Mum?

    B: **Thanks/Sorry, no**. I'm a bit busy.

3 **A:** Shall we go to the cinema tonight?

    B: **Yes, please/That's a good idea**. What's on?

4 **A:** How about eating salad tonight?

    B: **Of course/No, thanks**. I want chicken risotto.

5 **A:** Let's go swimming tomorrow.

    B: **No, let's not/you can't**. It's going to rain!

22 Put the words in order.

1 Can | use | I | pen? | your

2 go | Can | we | park | to the | after school?

3 we | Shall | homework | do | together? | our

4 going | How about | cinema? | to the

5 have | Let's | a | barbecue.

23 Look at 21 and 22. Ask and answer.

> No, thanks.   No, you can't.   OK. That's a good idea.
> Sorry, no.   Yes, of course.   Yes, you can.

Shall we do our homework together?

OK. That's a good idea.

24 Read and complete the sentences.

1 How about eating pasta for dinner? → Shall ❓ pasta for dinner?

2 I'd like to have a glass of milk, please. → Can ❓ a glass of milk, please?

3 Let's go to the cinema tonight. → Shall ❓ the cinema tonight?

4 Shall we have a cup of coffee? → How ❓ a cup of coffee?

School Lunches

Every day, children all over the world eat lunch at school. Some bring food from home, but many get their lunch from the school canteen. Let's take a look at what children in different countries around the world might be eating for lunch today.

1   In **Japan**, children eat lunch in their classroom. Pupils clear their desks, then four or five pupils take turns serving the food each day. Rice and soup are often part of school lunches in Japan. Some children bring boxes of cold rice, fish cakes and vegetables from home. They're carefully and beautifully prepared, because in Japan, the way food looks is very important.

2   In the **UK**, some schools provide hot lunches but most children bring a lunch box from home. Sandwiches with fillings such as cheese, ham or tuna are popular and there is often a piece of fruit, a bag of crisps, a carton of juice and a biscuit. Lunch is usually a small meal because dinner is the main meal of the day in the **UK**.

25 **Read and choose. Share your answers with the class.**

1   I eat lunch **at home/at school**.

2   Lunchtime is **before/after** one o' clock.

3   My lunch is usually a **hot/cold** meal.

4   My lunch comes from **home/the school canteen**.

5   Lunch **is/isn't** the most important meal of the day in my country.

26 **Read the article quickly and complete.**

	Japan	UK	Zambia	Italy
Cold lunch from home	✓	2	4	6
Hot meal	1	3	5	7

3   In **Zambia**, many children eat a dish called nshima for lunch. In fact, many people in Zambia often eat nshima for both lunch and dinner. Nshima is a sticky dough made from white ground maize. People eat nshima with their hands. They dip it into tasty sauces and usually eat it with some hot meat or fish.

4   In **Italy**, the food in school lunches is often organic, meaning it's grown naturally, without chemicals. This makes it healthier. The food also comes from farms near the schools. These hot lunches usually include pasta or a rice dish called risotto. Both pasta and risotto can be cooked in many different ways. Most schools in Italy serve meat only once or twice a week.

Hot, cold, big or small: School lunches are very different around the world. What's in yours today?

 53

27 Listen and read. Say the country or countries.

1 Children eat in their classroom.

2 Food is from a farm.

3 Children eat with their hands.

4 Children eat rice.

5 Lunch can be hot or cold.

6 There is something sweet with the meal.

7 Lunch and dinner are often the same.

28 Think about your lunch. Look, answer and write in your notebook.

1 Where do you eat?

2 When do you eat?

3 Who do you eat with?

4 What do you usually eat? Is it hot or cold?

My School Lunch

I usually eat lunch at school at twelve o'clock. It's a hot meal and I eat it in the school canteen with my friends. It's a small meal because dinner is more important in my country.

 THINK BIG Which lunchtime meal from the text is similar to yours? Why is it important to eat regularly?

55

29 **Complete the sentences. Use so or because. Then listen and check.**

We use so and because to connect sentences.

I like being healthy. I eat yoghurt and fruit for breakfast.
I like being healthy, so I eat yoghurt and fruit for breakfast.

I love eating watermelon. It's delicious.
I love eating watermelon, because it's delicious.

1 I like eating porridge for breakfast ❓ it's warm and yummy.

2 I like eating meat ❓ I often have lamb meatballs.

30 **Join the sentences. Use the conjunction.**

1 My sister likes chicken curry. She eats it twice a week. (so)

2 I usually eat fruit in the morning. It's tasty. (because)

3 We can have Mexican food tonight. There's a new restaurant in town. (because)

4 I'm going to Spain next month. I'd like to try some paella. (so)

31 **Find the conjunctions.**

I like eating vegetables, so I eat them every day. I eat them, because they make me feel healthy and are good for my body. I also like drinking fruit juice, but I don't really like fruit, so I don't eat a lot of fruit. But, I love watermelon! Because I really love it, I sometimes eat it at lunch or dinner!

32 **In your notebook, write three sentences about food that you like or don't like. Use because and so.**

56
33 **Listen, read and repeat.**

1 le   2 el   3 al   4 il

57
34 **Listen and find. Then say.**

apple   **cam**el   **med**al   **pen**cil

58
35 **Listen and blend the sounds.**

1 b-u-bb-le   bubble   2 u-n-c-le   uncle
3 t-r-a-v-el   travel   4 a-p-r-il   April
5 s-a-n-d-al-s   sandals   6 t-o-w-el   towel
7 p-u-p-il   pupil   8 l-o-c-al   local

59
36 **Read aloud. Then listen and chant.**

> Take your pencil.
> Draw a camel.
> Draw a medal.
> Draw some bubbles.

37 Listen and complete. Use words from the box.

> apple   biscuits   cake   carrots   crisps   doughnuts   popcorn   yoghurt

1 I like ❓ but ❓ is healthier.

2 ❓ are delicious but they've got lots of sugar in them. I'll have an ❓.

3 I love ❓ but they're not very good for me. ❓ is better.

4 I had some ❓ last night. Today, I want to have some ❓ for a snack.

 38 Talk about choosing healthy foods with a partner.

 I like sweets but a banana is healthier.

I like ice cream but an orange is better.

PROJECT

 39 Make a Healthy Foods collage. Then present it to the class.

Healthy Foods

40 **Complete the dialogue.**

do (x2)   like (x3)   would (x3)

A: What ¹❓ you ²❓ to eat for lunch?

B: I'm not sure.

A: How about that new Thai restaurant? ³❓ you ⁴❓ to go there?

B: Yes, I ⁵❓ . What's Thai food like?

A: Some of it is spicy. ⁶❓ you ⁷❓ spicy food?

B: Yes, I ⁸❓ !

A: Great. Let's go.

41 **Make your own restaurant. First, make a menu for breakfast and lunch. Next, take food orders from your classmates. Write the orders.**

Ray's Restaurant

Breakfast

eggs and toast	€3.00
yoghurt and fruit	€3.50
cereal with milk	€2.75
porridge	€2.75
orange juice	€2.00
milk	€1.75

Lunch

noodle soup	€3.50
chicken curry	€5.25
paella	€4.95
toasted cheese sandwich	€4.50
burger and chips	€3.75
lemonade	€2.00

What would you like for breakfast?

I'd like some porridge, please.

How about a drink with that?

That's a good idea. Thank you. Can I have some juice, please?

I Can

- talk about what people eat.
- make polite requests.
- talk about a balanced diet.
- find and use *because* and *so*.

How Well Do I Know It? Can I Use It?

1 **Think about it. Read and draw. Practise.**

😊 I know this. 😐 I need more practice. ☹️ I don't know this.

		PAGES			
1	**Appearance:** tall, short, straight black hair…	4	😊	😐	☹️
2	**Personality:** friendly, funny, clever, shy, serious…	4	😊	😐	☹️
3	**Activities:** go to the dentist, go on holiday, visit my grandparents, have a guitar lesson…	20	😊	😐	☹️
4	**Expressions of frequency:** every day, once a week, three times a year…	21	😊	😐	☹️
5	**Food:** porridge, noodle soup, lamb meatballs, watermelon…	36	😊	😐	☹️
6	Chris is **taller than** Tom. Mary's backpack is **heavier than** Kim's. My sister's hair is longer than **my hair/mine**.	8–9	😊	😐	☹️
7	The blue T-shirt is **better/more expensive**. My Maths grade is **worse than** yours.	12–13	😊	😐	☹️
8	**What** are you doing on Friday? **How often** do you have a guitar lesson?	24–25	😊	😐	☹️
9	**I'm going to** wear this shirt. What **is** Sienna **going to** do?	28–29	😊	😐	☹️
10	What **would** you **like**? **I'd like** some porridge. **Would** she **like to try** some chicken curry? Yes, she **would**./No, she **wouldn't**.	40–41	😊	😐	☹️
11	**Can I** sit down? **Can you** help me? **Shall we** go? **How about** that bean soup? **Let's** eat here.	44–45	😊	😐	☹️

62

2 **Get ready.**

A Complete the dialogue. Then listen and check.

a Ms Hart's hair is shorter than Ms Roberts'.

b She's really nice.

c Ms Hart is going to bring pizza to class.

d Ms Hart brought some Indian vegetable curry to class.

e Can I come to your Social Science class tomorrow?

f Every Tuesday and Thursday.

Anna: Social Science is more interesting this year. Our new teacher is Ms Hart.

Dad: What's she like?

Anna: ¹ ⸮ . And she's funny, too!

Dad: Oh, I think I saw her! Has she got long blonde hair?

Anna: No, that's Ms Roberts. ² ⸮ . And Ms Hart wears glasses.

Dad: Interesting. When have you got Social Science?

Anna: ³ ⸮ . Right now we're learning about India. ⁴ ⸮ .

Dad: Really? Was it good?

Anna: Yeah. I loved it! Yesterday we learned about Spain and Ms Hart brought us paella. Tomorrow we're going to learn about Italy. ⁵ ⸮ .

Dad: That's fantastic! ⁶ ⸮ .

B Practise the dialogue in **A** with a partner.

C Ask and answer the questions with a partner.

1 Would you like to try the food in **A**?

2 What countries do you learn about in Social Science?

 **Get set.**

 STEP 1 Create information about someone you would like to have as a pen pal. What is he/she like? Where does he/she live?

 STEP 2 Cut out the book outline on page 157 of your Activity Book. Fold it to make a book.

 STEP 3 Write about your pen pal in your book. Now you're ready to **GO!**

4 Go!

A Swap books with three classmates. Write notes about their pen pals in your notebook. Ask and answer questions like the ones below.

- What are the pen pals' names?
- What are they like?/What do they look like?
- What do they like doing?
- What food do they like eating?

_____'s Pen Pal

Name:

Is like/Looks like:

Likes doing:

Likes eating:

B Tell your class about some of your group's pen pals.

Maria's pen pal lives in China. She likes watching films. She likes eating steamed buns.

5 **Write about yourself in your notebook.**

- Who is taller, you or your best friend?
- What is your best friend like?
- What does your best friend look like?

- How often do you play with your friends?
- What are you going to do this weekend?
- What food would you like to try?

All About Me
Date:_____

_____

_____

How Well Do I Know It Now?

6 **A** **Look at page 52 and your notebook. Draw again.**

   B **Use a different colour.**

   C **Read and think.**

   I can start the next unit.

   I can ask my teacher for help and then start the next unit.

   I can practise and then start the next unit.

7 **Rate this Checkpoint.**

 very easy   easy   hard   very hard   fun   OK   not fun

Units 1–3 Exam Preparation

– Part A –

 Listen and draw lines. There is one example.

Paul   Vicky   Sally   Lily

Charlie   Daisy   Jack

– Part B –

Look and read. Write *yes* or *no*.

Examples

It's a sunny day.

_____ *yes* _____

The man has got a moustache.

_____ *no* _____

1 The boy with dark hair would like a toasted cheese sandwich.

_____

2 The man has got straight black hair.

_____

3 The girl is carrying her backpack on her back.

_____

4 The boy in the red T-shirt is taller than the boy in the green T-shirt.

_____

5 The boys sitting in the car are serious.

_____

6 The advertisement is for a breakfast cereal.

_____

Unit 4
How Do You Feel?

64

1 Listen, look and say.

1 allergies

2 cough

3 fever

4 headache

5 cut

6 sneeze

7 sore throat

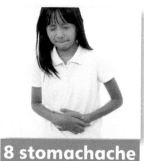
8 stomachache

9 cold

10 toothache

65

2 Listen, find and say.

3 Play a game.

4 Listen and sing. Who's speaking?

Stay in Bed and Rest!

You're coughing and
You're sneezing.
You need to stay in bed.
I think you've got a fever.
Here, let me feel your head.
You shouldn't go to
School today.
You should stay
Home instead.

**When you're ill or feeling blue,
Your family takes good care
Of you.**

You've got a fever and
A cold.
Here's what I suggest:
You should drink some tea
And juice.
Stay in bed and rest!
Listen to your dad, now.
Taking care of yourself
Is best.

Chorus

5 Read and choose.

1 Ben has got **bad stomachache/a bad headache**. He ate something bad last night.

2 Philip fell and hurt himself on the playground. He's got a big **fever/cut** on his knee.

3 It's spring and Pablo has got terrible **allergies/cuts**. He's **sore throat/sneezing**.

4 Karen's teeth are sore and she can't eat. She's got a terrible **headache/ toothache**.

5 Sandra has got a bad **cold/cut**. She's **allergies/coughing** and she's got a **sore throat/sneezing**. She has to stay home from school.

6 Meral has got a terrible **fever/stomachache** and **headache/cut**. She's very hot and her throat is sore.

THINK BIG Read and say what's wrong.

1 The trees are making Batu sneeze.

2 Emma is bleeding.

Story

6 **Listen and read. Does Christina need a nurse?**

1 Sam and Christina are eating lunch together at school. Christina's got a problem.

2 Sam gets upset when he sees Christina's arm. He thinks she cut herself.

3 Sam wants to help Christina.

4 Christina doesn't need to go to the nurse. She's OK.

5   Christina cleans her arm.

6   Now Sam doesn't feel very well.

7   **Who says it? Say Sam or Christina.**

1   "You've got a cut."
2   "You should see the school nurse!"
3   "I don't need a nurse."
4   "You should put a plaster on that."
5   "I just need a napkin!"
6   "You shouldn't worry so much!"

THINK BIG   Why did Sam get upset? Why didn't Christina get upset?
What should you do if you cut yourself?

70

8 Listen and look at the sentences. Help Sam and Christina make more.

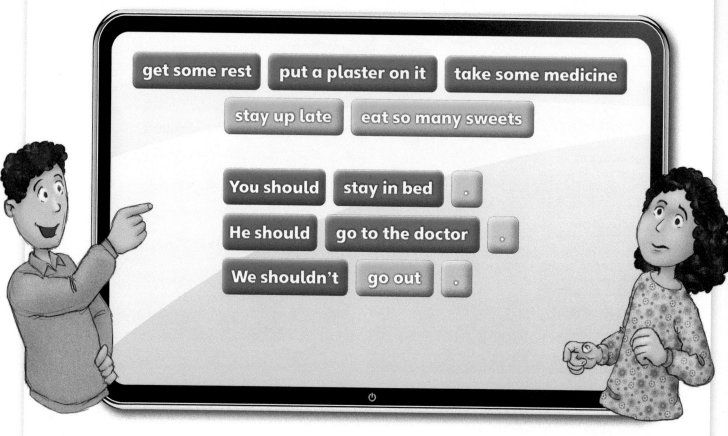

| get some rest | put a plaster on it | take some medicine |

| stay up late | eat so many sweets |

You should | stay in bed | .

He should | go to the doctor | .

We shouldn't | go out | .

9 Complete with should or shouldn't.

1 **A:** I've got stomachache.

   B: You ？ eat so many sweets.

2 **A:** He's got a toothache.

   B: He ？ go to the dentist.

3 **A:** They've got colds.

   B: They ？ stay in bed and drink a lot of water.

4 **A:** Mary feels ill.

   B: She ？ go out and play. She ？ go to bed.

10 Role play with a partner.

He's got a cut.

He should go to the nurse.

11 **Read. Then complete the sentences.**

I	myself
you	yourself
he	himself
she	herself
we	ourselves
they	themselves

I should take better care of myself.	My sister should take better care of ¹❓.
We take good care of ourselves.	They take good care of ²❓.

12 **Complete and match.**

1 My dad eats a healthy breakfast.
2 My sister stays up very late.
3 We always wash our hands.
4 He's got a cut on his arm.

a He should take better care of ❓.
b We take good care of ❓.
c She should take better care of ❓.
d He takes good care of ❓.

13 **Read and write in your notebook. Use take good care of or should take better care of.**

1 I eat too many sweets.
2 My sister often goes to bed late.
3 My brother exercises every day.
4 My family eat healthy food.
5 You're hurt.
6 My grandparents are 80.

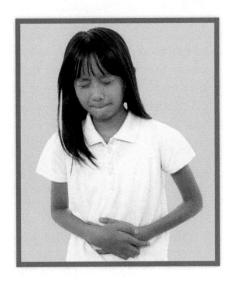

14 **Read and choose. Then say why. Collect ideas in your class.**

1 You **should/shouldn't** use a tissue when you sneeze.

2 You **should/shouldn't** wash your hands before you eat.

3 You **should/shouldn't** drink water from a lake.

4 You **should/shouldn't** go to school if you are ill.

72
 15 **Listen and read. Check your answers in 14. Are your reasons the same or different?**

CONTENT WORDS

bacteria disease enemy fever fungi germ malaria
microscope protect protozoa spread virus vomit

Germs

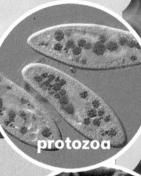
protozoa

1 Our bodies work hard to stay healthy but there are many tiny enemies around us that can make us ill. They're called germs. We can't see germs with our eyes – we can only see them through a microscope. When they're inside us, they use our body's resources and take away our energy. Germs can cause fever, coughing and other problems, so it's important to stay away from them as much as we can.

2 There are four main kinds of germs: bacteria, viruses, fungi and protozoa. They live in different places but they can all make us ill. Viruses are in the air. When we get a cough or a cold, it usually comes from a virus. The virus spreads through our bodies and then spreads to other people through the air. If you sneeze and you don't use a tissue, the virus goes into the air. This is why you shouldn't go to school with a bad cough or cold.

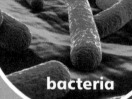
bacteria

3 Bacteria and fungi live in the air, too but they also grow on things, such as old food. This is why we should keep food in the fridge. When we eat bad bacteria or fungi, we get stomachache or we vomit. However, not all bacteria are bad. There are important bacteria in our stomachs, too. We use them to digest our food.

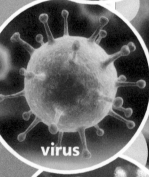
virus

4 Protozoa can also give you stomachache. Protozoa like wet places and can live in dirty water. This is why you should never drink water from a river or a lake. The disease malaria comes from protozoa. It lives in mosquitoes.

5 How can we stay away from germs? Unfortunately, our homes are perfect places for them because there are lots of places to hide. How can we protect ourselves? We can try to be cleaner but because we can't clean everything, we should wash our hands regularly and especially before we eat.

fungi

16 **Look at 15. Read and choose.**

1 We can see germs...   **a** with our eyes.   **b** with a microscope.

2 Germs take away our body's...   **a** bacteria.   **b** energy.

3 Bacteria, fungi, viruses and protozoa are all...   **a** germs.   **b** poisons.

4 Viruses...   **a** aren't dangerous.   **b** can spread very quickly.

5 Some bacteria...   **a** help our bodies.   **b** live in wet places.

6 We should always...   **a** try to be clean.   **b** protect our hands.

17 **Look at 15. Complete the chart.**

	Virus	Bacteria and fungi	3 ⸮
Where?	1 ⸮	In the air On food and surfaces	4 ⸮
What does it do?	Causes coughs and colds	2 ⸮	Causes malaria
What should you do?	Don't go to school if you're ill	Don't eat old food	5 ⸮

THINK BIG **Which germs in the text are most dangerous for us? Why?**

PROJECT

18 **Make a Stay Healthy poster. Then present it to the class.**

1 Choose a place: kitchen, bathroom, classroom or your own idea.

2 Write your Stay Healthy rules.

3 Put your poster on the wall. How many different rules are there?

Stay Healthy in the Kitchen!

✔ Wash your hands before you start to cook.

✔ Always clean the table after you eat.

74

19 **Listen and read. What does Mikey want to do?**

Mikey and Leo are brothers. It's three o'clock in the morning and Leo is scared.

Leo: Hey, Mikey, wake up!

Mikey: Hmm? Leo?

Leo: Mikey! Listen! I can hear strange noises. Maybe we should wake Mum and Dad. Should we go downstairs? Should we call the police?

Mikey: Don't be silly. No, we shouldn't!

Leo: Well, what should we do?

Mikey: What should you do, you mean? Well first, you could stop shaking me. And second, you could let me sleep! And third, you could put that noisy cat outside. Then you could go back to sleep and be quiet!

20 **Look at 19. Complete the charts.**

Should I/you/he/she/it/we/they eat?	What ¹ 🔲 we do? **Should** we ² 🔲 downstairs? ³ 🔲 the police?	Yes, we **should**. No, we ⁴ 🔲 .

I/you/he/she/it/we/they **could** go out.	You ⁵ 🔲 stop shaking me. You ⁶ 🔲 that noisy cat outside. We **could** tell Mum and Dad.

21 **Read. Make questions and short answers with should/shouldn't.**

1 **A:** I've got an exam tomorrow morning. 🔲 (stay up/I) late? **B:** 🔲

2 **A:** Dad's car isn't working. 🔲 (take/he) it to a mechanic? **B:** 🔲

3 **A:** Susan has got a bad toothache. 🔲 (go/she) to the dentist? **B:** 🔲

4 **A:** It's dinner time. 🔲 (wash/we) our hands? **B:** 🔲

5 **A:** Teresa and her sister have got bad coughs. 🔲 (go/they) to school today? **B:** 🔲

22 Look at **21** again. Make suggestions with **could** and match.

a Or she 🔔 (take) a pill.

b But they 🔔 (do) their school project at home.

c Or he 🔔 (fix) it himself.

d You 🔔 (set) your alarm, too.

e You 🔔 (clean) the table, too.

23 Write the questions in the right order in your notebook.

1 It's a rainy weekend in London. should What we do?

2 It's sunny in Brighton! Where go should swimming? we

3 should What I do bad stomachache? for

4 for exams? How I should study

5 put should we old medicine? Where

24 Look at **23**. Ask and answer the questions. Use **could** and these ideas.

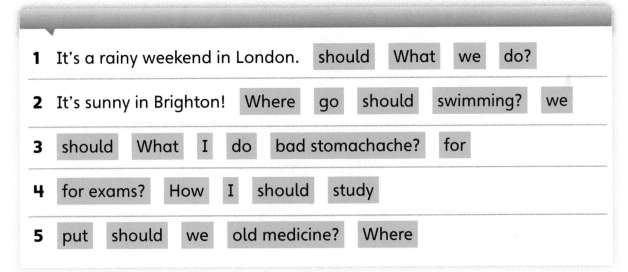

Visit the Barbican Indoor Garden!

SAFE BIN –
Put your old
medicines in here

Visit Brighton Beach for a day in the sun!

Call us for help with revision – Revise Right!

Give your medicine back to us –
Caring Chemist's

Visit the British Museum –
Fun on a rainy day!

I'm Katie Miller. Call me – I can
help you with your schoolwork.

Take EasyTum – feel better fast

a

b

Home Remedies

1 Should you see a doctor every time you're ill? Of course not! Doctors haven't got a cure for everything. In fact, there are many simple illnesses that are difficult for doctors to cure. Sometimes people use different "home remedies" for them.

2 The cold virus is one example. People in many countries don't take medicine for a cold – they make a big pot of hot chicken soup instead. They eat the soup and rest. Many people believe that chicken soup is a natural and healthy cure for a cold. And in fact, it really helps: drinking a lot of water is good when you've got a cold. Also, the hot soup helps you breathe better and eases your sore throat.

25 **Read the problems. What could they do? Discuss with a partner.**

Bill: I've got a bad cold. I can't breathe. Yuk!

Tammy: I've got stomachache. It's horrible! What could I eat or drink?

Laura: This headache is really bad but I don't want to take medicine. Can you help me?

Kemal: My throat is really sore! What could I do to feel better?

Bill could drink orange juice.
It's got vitamin C in it.

26 **Read the article quickly. What does it say? Choose one.**

1 Home remedies aren't very good.

2 Doctors can cure everything.

3 Some home remedies help you feel better.

4 People should always use home remedies.

5 Home remedies are the same around the world.

27 **Look again. What are the things in pictures a–d good for?**

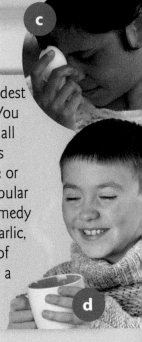

3 If you've got a headache, your doctor may give you painkillers. However, in China, it's common to cure a headache with an egg! You boil the egg, take off the shell and rub the egg on your face, head and neck until the egg becomes cool. Some people think this helps you sleep better, too. Rubbing with the egg relaxes you, like a massage. Often headaches are because of stress, so relaxing is a good idea.

4 What about a fever? There are lots of different home remedies but one interesting home remedy uses vinegar. In Russia, people rub vinegar into the skin. The vinegar makes your skin feel cooler and it can help lower your body temperature a little.

5 One of the world's oldest home remedies is tea. You can use herbal teas for all sorts of simple illnesses such as a stomachache or a sore throat. Some popular ingredients in home remedy teas are mint, ginger, garlic, honey and lemon. All of these ingredients make a sore throat feel better and help you relax.

 75

28 Listen and read. Complete the sentences.

> cooler cure herbal massage painkillers rest stress

1 Doctors don't have a ❓ for all illnesses.
2 When people have got a cold, they often eat chicken soup and ❓.
3 Doctors give ❓ for headaches.
4 When you rub the egg on your head, it feels like a ❓.
5 Often headaches are because of ❓.
6 When you put vinegar on your skin, it feels ❓.
7 People around the world use ❓ teas for many illnesses.

29 Create a fact file for a home remedy. Use a remedy you know or a remedy in the article. Use this fact file to help you.

Problem: Sore throat	
What can you use?	Garlic in warm water.
Where did you find it?	My grandma uses it.
Why does it work?	It kills bad bacteria and helps the pain.

 THINK BIG Do people use these home remedies in your country? Are home remedies better than doctors and medicine? Why/Why not?

30 **Read and choose the sentences where commas are used correctly.**

We use a comma (,) between items in a list. We don't use a comma before and or or in a list.

1 I should rest, take medicine and drink tea.
2 I should rest, take medicine, and drink tea.

We use a comma after most sequence words. We don't use a comma after Then.

1 First I brush my teeth. Then, I wash my hands.
2 First, I brush my teeth. Then I wash my hands.

We use a comma before too at the end of a sentence.

1 He should put a plaster on his cut and go to the nurse, too.
2 He should put a plaster on his cut and go to the nurse too.

31 **Copy the paragraph in your notebook. Put commas in the correct places.**

Here's how I take care of myself and stay healthy. First I exercise every day. I run play football ride my bike and do gymnastics. I like skateboarding too. Next I only eat healthy food. I eat fruit vegetables and yoghurt. I don't eat unhealthy foods like crisps doughnuts or chips. I try to protect myself from germs too. I wash my hands take showers and brush my teeth. Finally I get enough rest and I go to bed early every night.

32 **How do you take care of yourself? Write a paragraph in your notebook.**

33 **Listen, read and repeat.**

1 kn

2 wr

34 **Listen and find. Then say.**

knee

write

35 **Listen and blend the sounds.**

1 kn-ow	know	**2** wr-o-ng	wrong
3 wr-a-p	wrap	**4** kn-o-ck	knock
5 kn-igh-t	knight	**6** wr-i-s-t	wrist
7 kn-o-t	knot	**8** wr-e-ck	wreck

36 **Read aloud. Then listen and chant.**

What's wrong, wrong, wrong?
The knight knocked his
Knee, knee, knee
And his wrist, wrist, wrist.
I know! Wrap his knee
And wrap his wrist!

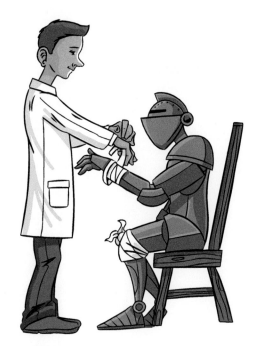

82

 Listen and say the letter.

a You should cough or sneeze into the inside of your arm.

b You should wash your hands often.

c You shouldn't share food, cups, forks or spoons.

38 **Tell a partner how you can stop spreading germs.**

I wash my hands many times a day.

PROJECT

39 **Make a Good Hygiene Habits checklist. Compare your checklist with a partner's.**

Name _____

Good Hygiene Habits

 **Wash your hands.** ☐

 **Cough or sneeze into your arm.** ☐

 **Don't share food, cups, forks or spoons.** ☐

40 **Complete the dialogues.**

> allergies   cold   cut   exercise   plaster
> should   shouldn't   stomachache   sweets   themselves

1 **A:** Oh, no. I've got a ❓ .

   B: You should put a ❓ on it.

2 **A:** They do ❓ every day.

   B: They take good care of ❓ .

3 **A:** My sister has got ❓ .

   B: She shouldn't eat so many ❓ .

4 **A:** His ❓ are really bad today.

   B: He ❓ take some medicine and stay in the house.

5 **A:** I've got a ❓ .

   B: You ❓ go to school today.

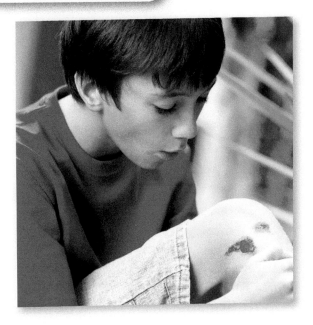

41 **Role play giving advice with a partner.**

I've got a very bad toothache. What should I do?

I could go to a dentist.

You should see a doctor.

Yes, you could ask Mum to take you.

I Can

- talk about illnesses and health problems.
- ask and give advice and make suggestions.
- talk about different kinds of germs.
- use commas correctly.

Unit 5 Weird and Wild Animals

1 **Listen, look and say.**

1 Tasmanian devil

Lives in: Australia
Population: between 10,000 and 25,000

2 Andean condor

Lives in: South America
Population: about 10,000

3 angler fish

Lives in: oceans all over the world
Population: we don't know

4 volcano rabbit

Lives on: volcanoes in Mexico
Population: between 2,000 and 12,000

5 coconut crab

Lives on: islands in the Pacific Ocean
Population: more than 100,000

6 tarsier

Lives in: Southeast Asia
Population: we don't know

2 **Listen, find and say.**

3 **Play a game.**

4 **Listen and sing. Why is it important to learn about animals?**

Understanding Animals

Do you know a lot about animals?
How many different kinds there are?
Some are big and some are small
And some are just bizarre!

**Understanding animals is good for us to do
Because learning about animals helps us
And helps them, too!**

Some live in trees or in the sea
And some live where it's hot.
Some are beautiful and some are cute
And some are... well, they're not!

Chorus

It's important to learn about animals,
Though many seem strange, it's true.
Because when we learn about animals,
We learn about ourselves, too.

Chorus

5 **Ask and answer about the animals in** 1.

> Where do coconut crabs live?

> They live on islands in the Pacific Ocean.

> How many are there?

> There are more than 100,000.

THINK BIG **Find a photo of another weird animal. Tell the class about its population and where it lives.**

6 **Listen and read. What is the programme about?**

Chimps Are Clever!

Wow! Chimpanzees are amazing animals. They can talk to each other!

1 Christina is watching a TV programme about chimpanzees or chimps. She's telling Sam about them.

They can climb trees and they know how to use tools, too!

Really?

2 Christina explains that chimps make tools to get food.

Oh, no! That's sad. Chimps are endangered.

3 Christina finds out that chimps are endangered.

A hundred years ago, there were more than one million chimps. But now there are only 200,000.

100 years ago   Today

4 The programme says that there are not many chimps left.

5 Christina explains that people move in and destroy the jungle and the chimps have nowhere to live.

6 Sam laughs at Christina's joke.

7 **Look at the story. Ask and answer.**

1 What things can chimps do?

2 How many chimps were there 100 years ago?

3 How many are there now?

4 Why are chimps endangered?

5 Is Sam endangered?

THINK BIG **What other animals are endangered and why?**
What can we do to help them?

Language in Action

89

8 Listen and look at the sentences. Help Sam and Christina make more.

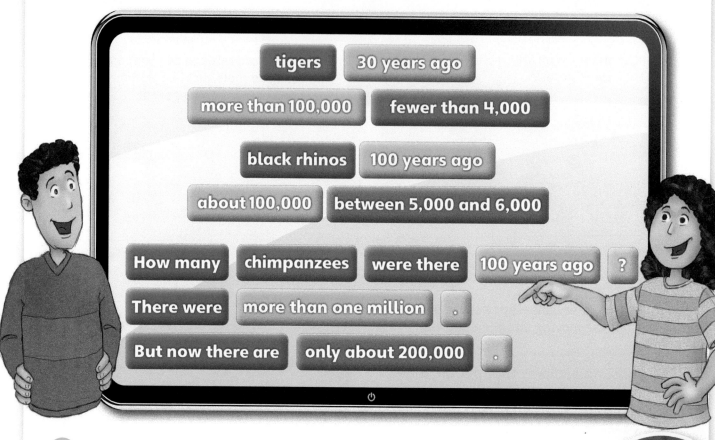

tigers   30 years ago

more than 100,000   fewer than 4,000

black rhinos   100 years ago

about 100,000   between 5,000 and 6,000

How many   chimpanzees   were there   100 years ago   ?

There were   more than one million   .

But now there are   only about 200,000   .

9 Complete the sentences.

1 ❓ Komodo dragons were there 50 years ago?

❓ more than 20,000. But now ❓ probably fewer than 5,000 in the Komodo Islands.

2 ❓ Andean condors were there in the past?

❓ many Andean condors in the mountains of South America. But now ❓ about 10,000.

3 ❓ Asian elephants were there 100 years ago?

❓ about 90,000 throughout Asia. But now ❓ about 45,000.

4 ❓ Tasmanian devils were there 25 years ago?

❓ more than 100,000 Tasmanian devils. But now ❓ between 10,000 and 25,000.

10 **Read. Then complete the sentences.**

Why are Andean flamingos endangered?	They're endangered because their habitat's polluted.
¹ ？ are chimpanzees endangered?	They're endangered ² ？ people are destroying their habitat.
³ ？ are tigers endangered?	They're endangered ⁴ ？ people are killing them.

11 **Ask and answer about why each animal is endangered.**

1 why/coconut crabs/endangered

People are eating them./People are destroying their habitat.

2 why/Andean condors/endangered

Other animals are killing them./They're getting ill and dying.

3 why/volcano rabbits/endangered

People are destroying their habitat./There's too much pollution.

4 why/Tasmanian devils/endangered

People are killing them./People are moving into their habitat.

5 why/black rhinos/endangered

People are killing them./People are destroying their habitat.

12 **Work with a partner to find out more about the animals on pages 78 and 79. Discuss.**

13 Look at the animals in the pictures. Do you know their names? Which animals live in your country?

a

b

c

d

14 Listen and read. Match pictures **a–d** in **13** to paragraphs **1–4**.

CONTENT WORDS

cave   endangered   fur   in the wild   pond   predator   protect   trap

---

Strange and Endangered

Our world is beautiful but it's changing. For some wild animals, nowhere is safe in nature any more – hunting and disease mean they've got no home. Let's meet some cute and unusual animals and find out why they're endangered.

1 The smallest bat in the world (¹ Picture ?) is called the **bumblebee bat** because it's the same size as a bumblebee! Bumblebee bats live in caves in the forests of Thailand and Myanmar. They're endangered because each year farmers burn the forests where they live. Most scientists agree that there are only about 6,000 bumblebee bats left in the wild.

2 This funny-looking fish (² Picture ?) is called the **Mexican walking fish**. It's not really a fish – it's a kind of salamander. It's got legs, so it can move around on land. It lives in the streams and ponds near Mexico City but most of these ponds are now polluted and the Mexican walking fish is nearly extinct.

3 One cute endangered animal (³ Picture ?) is the **red panda**. Most red pandas live in mountains in China, Myanmar and Nepal. They live in trees with red moss on their branches so they can hide from their predators. People hunt them for their fur but they also fall into traps set by hunters. Scientists say that there are fewer than 10,000 red pandas left in the wild.

4 The **Egyptian tortoise** (⁴ Picture ?) is the smallest tortoise in the world. When fully grown, the Egyptian tortoise is only 10 centimetres long. They live in the desert. They're so unusual that everyone wants one as a pet. As a result, there are fewer than 7,500 left in the wild now.

If we don't do something to protect these animals, they'll disappear. Then nothing will bring them back.

15 **Look at 14. Say the animal.**

1 It's a very popular pet.

2 It lives in caves in the forest.

3 Its colour helps it hide from predators.

4 It's almost extinct.

16 **Look at 14 and complete the cards about the animals. Then make sentences.**

a

> **Name:** Egyptian tortoise
>
> **Habitat:** deserts in Egypt
>
> **Number left in the wild:** fewer than **1** 🔑
>
> **Why endangered:** people want them as pets

b

> **Name:** Mexican walking fish
>
> **Habitat:** **2** 🔑 near Mexico City
>
> **Number left in the wild:** almost **3** 🔑
>
> **Why endangered:** ponds are **4** 🔑

c

> **Name:** red panda
>
> **Habitat:** **5** 🔑 in **6** 🔑 , Myanmar and Nepal
>
> **Number left in the wild:** fewer than **7** 🔑
>
> **Why endangered:** people destroying their habitat

d

> **Name:** bumblebee bat
>
> **Habitat:** **8** 🔑 in forests in Thailand and Myanmar
>
> **Number left in the wild:** about **9** 🔑
>
> **Why endangered:** farmers **10** 🔑 their habitat

Many scientists believe there are only about 6,000 bumblebee bats left in the wild.

Most bumblebee bats live in Thailand.

THINK BIG **How can people protect endangered animals?**

PROJECT

17 **Make an Endangered Animal fact file. Present it to the class.**

Aye-ayes are endangered because many people believe they're bad luck...

The Aye-aye

Name: Aye-aye

Habitat: Rain forests of Madagascar

Interesting fact: Uses a long middle finger to catch insects

Number left in wild: We don't know

Why endangered: People killing them because they think they're bad luck

93

18 Listen and read. Who took Ian's camera?

Ian and Lisa are looking at photos.

Ian: Look at my photos from the trip to the safari park.

Lisa: This elephant is great! Could you touch them?

Ian: No, we couldn't, but we were in a jeep, so we could go quite close. Look, these are the monkeys. They were really naughty.

Lisa: Naughty? Why? What did they do?

Ian: I tried to take a photo and they took my camera! I couldn't get it back.

Lisa: Where is it now?

Ian: At home. A park ranger gave it to me later.

 19 Look at **18**. Complete the charts.

I/you/he/she/it/we/they **could** play.	We **¹** go quite close.
I/you/he/she/it/we/they **couldn't** swim.	I **couldn't ²** it back.
Could I/you/he/she/it/we/they take a photo?	**³** you **⁴** them?
	Yes, we **could**.
	No, we **⁵** .

Who are they?	Ian and Lisa.
What could you see?	The monkeys.
⁶ were the monkeys naughty?	Because they took my camera.
When was the safari?	In March.
⁷ is it now?	At home.

We were in a jeep, **⁸** we could go quite close.
It's raining, **so** we can't go out.

20 **Complete the sentences. Use could or couldn't.**

1 Mehmet 🔋 speak English, so he talked to the tourists.
2 It was hot, so I 🔋 stay in the car.
3 🔋 you swim when you were six?
4 It was dark, so we 🔋 see.
5 I had my camera, so I 🔋 take lots of photos.
6 The weather was very bad, so we 🔋 have a picnic.
7 We finished all the exercises, so we 🔋 leave the lesson early.

21 **Look and complete the chart for you. Then discuss with a partner.**

What could you do five years ago?

	Keira	**Mike**	**You**
Read	✓	✗	
Ride a bike	✓	✓	
Use a computer	✗	✗	

Mike could ride a bike but he couldn't read.

Could Keira read five years ago?

Could you use a computer five years ago?

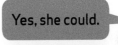

Yes, she could.

No, I couldn't.

22 **Read and match the words from the box.**

What? (x2)   When?   Where?   Who?   Why?

1 The elephant's name was…
2 I could understand the tourist because…
3 …was in the car with us.
4 Feeding time was at… o'clock.
5 The camera was in…
6 A bumblebee bat is…

23 **Look at 22. Write the questions in your notebook. Then write answers and compare with a partner.**

Dragons

1   Dragons are mythical creatures. That means they aren't real. They're important in many cultures around the world. People from North America, South America, Europe, Africa, Oceania and Asia talk about them in myths and fairy tales. However, different cultures see dragons quite differently.

2   In Asia, dragons are beautiful and magical creatures and some stories about them are more than 4,000 years old. Asian dragons haven't got wings. They look like giant lizards but they aren't scary – they help people and they can bring someone good luck. One example is Fuku Riu, the Japanese lucky dragon.

24 **What do you know about dragons? Think and make sentences.**

breathe fire   cave   eat   story   tail   wings

What can many dragons do?

In Europe, the stories say that they breathe fire.

25 **Read the article quickly and complete the chart.**

Name	Where from?	Real or mythical?	Scary?
Fuku Riu	1 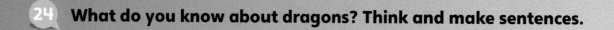	Mythical	2
The Bunyip	Australia and Oceania	3	4
The Komodo Dragon	5	6	Yes

3   In Europe, North America and South America, though, stories about dragons usually show them as evil. Western fairy-tale dragons live in caves. They've got giant wings and breathe fire, so they're usually scary! However, there are some stories about good dragons in Western culture.

4   Dragons also have a very long history in Australia and Oceania. Some of the dragon myths there are more than 50,000 years old. There are many different types of dragon but the most famous of all is the bunyip. This scary mythical monster is made from parts of different animals. It lives in the water and eats animals and sometimes people.

5   The only real dragon alive today is the Komodo dragon, a very large lizard that lives on an island in Indonesia. It can be scary because it hunts and eats almost anything: deer, pigs, other smaller dragons and even big animals and humans! The Komodo dragon is now an endangered species because of predators and changes to its habitat, so people are trying to help save it from extinction.

94

26   **Listen and read. Say True or False. Correct the false sentences.**

1   People all over the world see dragons.
2   Asian dragons look like giant lizards with wings.
3   In Asia, dragons are lucky creatures.
4   All European dragons are bad.
5   The bunyip looks very different from Asian dragons.
6   The Komodo dragon sometimes eats people.

27   **Look at the example. Create a fact file for a mythical or fairy-tale animal or monster. Find a picture or draw. Use this fact file to help you.**

Name:	Unicorn
What it looks like:	Beautiful white horse with a horn
About it:	Its horn can make ill people better.
Habitat:	Forests
Stories come from:	Different cultures

THINK BIG   **Do you know any myths or fairy tales about dragons? What are they?**

28 **Read and choose the correct end mark for each sentence.**

A sentence may end with a full stop (.), a question mark (?) or an exclamation mark (!). These are called end marks.

Use a full stop at the end of a sentence that makes a statement.
   I like stories about dragons.

Use a question mark at the end of a question.
   Why are tigers endangered?

Use an exclamation mark at the end of a statement which shows a strong feeling.
   The Komodo dragon is very scary!

1 How many Tasmanian devils were there in 1920   . / ? / !
2 People are moving into the forest   . / ? / !
3 Angler fish are very strange   . / ? / !
4 Do you like elephants   . / ? / !
5 Mexican walking fish lived in ponds   . / ? / !

29 **Rewrite each sentence in your notebook. Use a full stop, a question mark or an exclamation mark.**

1 There are many people that help endangered animals
2 Look at those fantastic dragons
3 Can frogs swim
4 Where do Komodo dragons live
5 Tarsiers are so cute
6 There were more than 100,000 tigers in the 1900s
7 What colour are Andean condors
8 We can do a lot to help endangered animals

30 **Write sentences in your notebook. Write one with a full stop, one with a question mark and one with an exclamation mark.**

96

31 **Listen, read and repeat.**

1 ph

2 wh

 97

32 **Listen and find. Then say.**

phone

whale

 98

33 **Listen and blend the sounds.**

1	ph-o-t-o	photo	**2** ph-a-n-t-o-m	phantom
3	wh-ea-t	wheat	**4** d-o-l-ph-i-n	dolphin
5	wh-i-te	white	**6** e-l-e-ph-a-n-t	elephant
7	wh-ee-l	wheel	**8** wh-e-n	when

99

34 **Read aloud. Then listen and chant.**

The phantom's got a photo
On his phone
Of a white wheel
And some wheat.

35 Listen and say the letter. Match the sentences in the box to the correct pictures.

> Don't pollute animal habitats.   Make space for wildlife.
> Reduce, reuse, recycle.

a

b

c

36 Discuss what you can do to help take care of animals and their habitats.

What can we do to protect endangered species?

How can we protect their habitats?

We can protect their habitats.

We can make space for wildlife.

PROJECT

37 Make Conservation signs. Post your signs in the halls of your school.

38 **Complete. Use words from the box.**

1   I missed the party. 🔑 was it?

2   I 🔑 eat because I was ill.

3   Derin 🔑 study later, so she went out.

4   She had school, 🔑 she didn't come.

> could   couldn't   so   When

39 **Ask and answer about these endangered animals.**

Name: Asian elephant
100 years ago: 90,000
Now: 45,000
Why endangered: People are killing them.

Name: Black rhino
100 years ago: 100,000
Now: between 5,000 and 6,000
Why endangered: People are killing them.

Name: Tasmanian devil
25 years ago: more than 100,000
Now: between 10,000 and 25,000
Why endangered: People are moving into their habitat.

Name: Tiger
100 years ago: more than 100,000
Now: fewer than 4,000
Why endangered: People are killing them.

How many tigers were there 100 years ago?

How many are there now?

Why are they endangered?

There were more than 100,000.

There are fewer than 4,000.

Because people are killing them.

I Can

- talk about animals and why some are endangered.
- ask questions and talk about abilities.
- use end marks correctly.

Life Long Ago

102

1 Listen, look and say.

NOW

1 travel by car

2 wash clothes in a washing machine

3 have a mobile phone

4 have electric lights

5 cook in a microwave

6 listen to an mp3 player

LONG AGO

7 cooked on a coal stove

8 had a phone with an operator

9 travelled by horse and carriage

10 washed clothes by hand

11 had oil lamps

12 listened to the radio

103

2 Listen, find and say.

3 Play a game.

4 Listen and sing. How did people get water one hundred years ago?

In the Old Days

Life one hundred years ago
Was different, you see.
There were no computers
And there was no TV.

Life was different in the old days.
Life was different in so many ways.

Children used to get water
From pumps or wells outdoors.
Now we just turn on the tap
And out fresh water pours!

Chorus

Life was so much slower!
Few people had a car.
Children used to walk to school
And they walked very far!

Chorus

5 Choose. Then match the activities of today with activities from the past.

cook   have   listen   travel   wash clothes

1 by car
2 in a washing machine
3 electric lights
4 in a microwave
5 to an mp3 player

a cooked on a coal stove
b had oil lamps
c listened to the radio
d travelled by horse and carriage
e washed clothes by hand

THINK BIG What else is different now? Tell a partner.

Story

6 **Listen and read. Did Grandma have a microwave when she was a child?**

Life Was Nicer Then

Grandma, can you pass me the TV remote control?

Come on, Sam! You can get it yourself.

1 Sam is watching TV and doesn't want to get off the sofa.

But Grandma...

Listen, Sam. When I was a child, we didn't have remote controls.

2 Grandma doesn't want Sam to be lazy.

What did you use to do?

We used to get up, walk to the TV and change the channel.

3 Most TVs didn't have remote controls when Sam's grandma was a child.

Did you have a lot of channels?

No, we didn't. We only had three channels. Oh, life was so simple, so quiet back then...

4 Sam's grandma thinks life was a lot nicer when she was young.

5 But now Sam's grandma sometimes uses a microwave to make dinner.

6 Maybe some things about modern life are nicer!

7 **Read and choose.**

When Sam's grandma was a child...

1 people **watched/didn't watch** TV.

2 people **had/didn't have** remote controls to change channels.

3 people **used/didn't use** to get up to change the channels.

4 life **was/wasn't** simpler and quieter.

5 people **used/didn't use** to cook in a microwave.

THINK BIG Has your family got a lot of remote controls?
What are they for?
What other modern technology makes life easier?

108

8 Listen and look at the sentences. Help Sam and Christina make more.

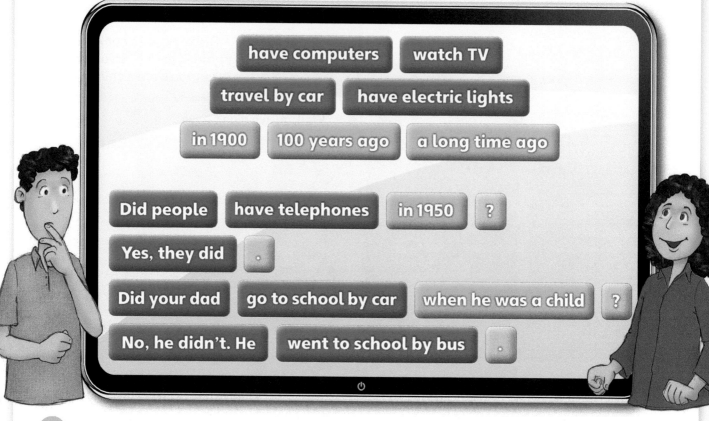

9 Complete the questions and answers.

1 ⸮ your mum ⸮ a car when she was at school?
   ⸮ . She had a bike.

2 ⸮ people ⸮ video games 20 years ago?
   ⸮ . There were some very popular video games back then.

3 ⸮ your grandad ⸮ a computer when he was a child?
   ⸮ . There were no computers then.

4 ⸮ people ⸮ taps in their homes 200 years ago?
   ⸮ . They got water from a pump outdoors.

10 Write the questions in the right order in your notebook. Then answer.

a mobile phones Did have people in 1900?

b your friends mp3 players listen to last year? Did

c your mum go to school Did by horse and carriage?

d wash Did people clothes by hand a long time ago?

11 Read. Then choose **use to** or **used to**.

My grandad used to walk to school.	He didn't use to ride a bike.
People ¹ 🔑 cook on coal stoves.	They didn't ² 🔑 cook in microwaves.
Did people use to listen to mp3 players?	No, they didn't. They used to listen to the radio.
Before cars, what did people ³ 🔑 do for transportation?	They ⁴ 🔑 travel by horse and carriage.
Before computers, how did people ⁵ 🔑 keep in touch?	They ⁶ 🔑 write letters.

12 Make sentences with **used to** (✔) and **didn't use to** (✗).

1 my dad/travel by car/✔
2 my grandma/have a mobile phone/✗
3 people/wash clothes in a washing machine/✗
4 my sister/watch films/✔
5 my brother/play video games/✔
6 people/listen to mp3 players/✗

13 Read the questions and answer them with your own ideas.

1 Before taps, how did people use to get water?
2 Before electric lights, what did people use to have?
3 Before TVs, what did people use to do at night?

14 Ask and answer.

Did people use to have computers a hundred years ago?

No, they didn't. They used to write letters to keep in touch.

 15 How fast do these things go, on average? Guess, then check with the class.

1 Somebody walking: **5/8** kilometres per hour

2 a horse and carriage: **8/15** kilometres per hour

3 a car in 1900: **25/40** kilometres per hour

4 a modern car: **90/110** kilometres per hour

 16 Listen and read. Check your answers in 15. Which one is not in the text?

CONTENT WORDS				
average speed	distance travelled	multiply	number of	per hour

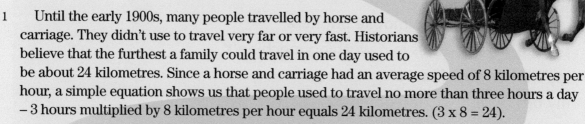

And Then There Were Cars

1   Until the early 1900s, many people travelled by horse and carriage. They didn't use to travel very far or very fast. Historians believe that the furthest a family could travel in one day used to be about 24 kilometres. Since a horse and carriage had an average speed of 8 kilometres per hour, a simple equation shows us that people used to travel no more than three hours a day – 3 hours multiplied by 8 kilometres per hour equals 24 kilometres. (3 x 8 = 24).

2   The distances people travelled changed in 1886, when Mr Karl Benz from Germany put an engine on a carriage. It was the first petrol-powered vehicle. Then in 1901, the German company Daimler Motors (DMG) created a beautiful motor car for racing. It was called the Mercedes. Its engine was lighter, so it could travel faster than any other car. The Mercedes also looked very different to the horse-drawn carriage. It was more attractive and it was safer because it was lower and closer to the road. Six Mercedes raced in Nice in 1901, reaching an average speed of 51 kilometres per hour.

3   Unfortunately, the Mercedes was expensive. It was, and it still is, a luxury. The average working man in America in the 1900s could not buy one. Henry Ford changed this when he built the Model T or "Tin Lizzie" in 1908. It was one of the first popular cars and people could buy it for about 850 dollars. All of a sudden, the number of cars on the road multiplied! Its average speed was about 40 kilometres per hour.

4   Modern cars today are much faster than they used to be in the past. The average speed of the modern car is about 90 kilometres per hour. However in big cities, because of all the traffic, we still don't travel much faster than we used to with the horse and carriage, all those years ago.

17 **Look at 16. Say True or False. Correct the sentences that are false.**

1 In the 1900s, everybody had a horse and carriage.
2 The first petrol-powered vehicle was invented in 1901.
3 Karl Benz built the first Mercedes.
4 The Mercedes looked really good.
5 People bought the Model T because it was cheaper.
6 Today, car travel in cities is the same as in the past.

18 **Copy the chart. Read and complete. Then multiply the numbers to find the distances travelled.**

	average speed (km/h)	number of hours	distance travelled
1901 Mercedes	¹🗯 x	4	= ⁴🗯
Model T ford	²🗯 x	5	= ⁵🗯
Modern cars	³🗯 x	2	= ⁶🗯

19 **Read. Write the equation and answer in your notebook.**

1 A plane travels at an average speed of 885 kilometres per hour. How many kilometres can you travel on a six hour-flight?

2 A city bike in London travels at an average speed of 29 kilometres per hour. How many kilometres can it travel in three hours?

3 If a train on the New York subway travels at an average speed of 64 kilometres per hour, how many kilometres can it travel in 2 hours?

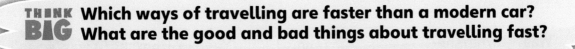

THINK BIG **Which ways of travelling are faster than a modern car?**
What are the good and bad things about travelling fast?

PROJECT

20 **Make a My Favourite Car fact file. Then present it to the class.**

Maker	Volkswagen
Engine cost	< than €20
Factory	Wolfsburg in Germany
In production	From 1945 to 1978
Units produced	21 million
Performance	+/– 96 kilometres per hour

21 Listen and read. What was Sophie doing at five o'clock yesterday?

Lucy and Sophie are talking.

Lucy: I phoned you at nine o'clock yesterday but you weren't at home. Where were you?

Sophie: I was running in the park with my mum at nine o'clock.

Lucy: What were you doing at eleven o'clock?

Sophie: I was at the sports centre with my sister. We were swimming.

Lucy: I called again at one o'clock.

Sophie: What was I doing at one o'clock? I wasn't swimming... Oh, yes! I was playing volleyball.

Lucy: At three o'clock?

Sophie: I was playing tennis with some friends.

Lucy: Were you still playing tennis at five o'clock? Beth and I were waiting for you at the cinema! You didn't come!

Sophie: Oh, I'm sorry! I was sleeping at five o'clock. I was exhausted!

22 Look at 21. Complete the charts.

✓	I/He/She/It	**was**	**swimming**.
	We/You/They	**were**	
✗	I/He/She/It	**wasn't**¹ 🔲	² 🔲 tennis.
	We/You/They	**weren't**	

Was	I/he/she/it	³ 🔲 tennis?	Yes/No, I/he/she/it **was/wasn't**.
⁴ 🔲	we/you/they	**sleeping**?	Yes/No, we/you/they **were/weren't**.

What	**was**	I/he/she/it	⁶ 🔲 at eleven o'clock?
	⁵ 🔲	we/you/they	

23 **Look at 22. Make questions. Write in your notebook.**

1 what/you/do/at/lunch time/yesterday?

2 your family/have/dinner/at eight o'clock/last night?

3 you/do/your homework/at half past six/on Sunday?

4 who/you/talk/to/before class/today?

5 what/you/watch/on TV/last night?

6 it/rain/at nine o'clock/this morning?

24 **Look at 23. Ask and answer with a partner.**

What were you doing at lunch time yesterday?

I was shopping in town!

25 **Complete the text.**

> ago   cleaning   didn't   drove   in   machine
> now   used   uses   washed   when

My grandfather's life is different now.
He ¹ to live in the city but now he
lives in the country. Many years ² , his
family ³ have a car, so they walked to
school and to the shops. ⁴ he's got a
car. ⁵ 1960, he ⁶ a car for the first
time! He was always ⁷ it. His mother
⁸ the clothes by hand and he helped.
But now he's got a washing ⁹ . ¹⁰ he

was younger, they didn't have a phone. Now he ¹¹ his mobile phone every
day. I think he prefers life now!

Living Traditionally in a Modern World

Could you live without a computer or a mobile phone? It might be hard for you to imagine a life without technology. But even today, many people all over the world live happily without it. There are many tribes with much more important things to worry about than technology.

26 **Which items of technology are really important for you? Work with a partner. Put the things in order of importance.**

> computer/laptop   cooker   Internet   mobile phone
> TV   washing machine

27 **Read the article quickly and complete.**

Name of tribe:	1	4	Koryak
Country:	Africa	5	7
Where they live:	2	hills and mountains	8
Way of life	3	6	hunting, fishing, cooking

One of the most famous tribes on the planet is the Maasai people of Kenya, in Africa. The Maasai are nomadic. This means they don't live in one place all the time. They move from place to place and make new homes each time they move. They build their homes in the forests from things they can find in nature – mud, sticks, grass and rocks. Their villages don't have running water or electricity, so computers and mobile phones are not an option.

Another tribe in South East Asia is The Hmong. These are hill people – they live in the mountains in parts of Thailand, Laos and Vietnam. They have a very traditional way of life. In fact, they live the same way now that their ancestors used to live over 2,000 years ago. They've also got their own ancient language with two different dialects;

Hmong Djua and Hmong Daw. The language comes from Southern China and it's quite different to the other languages of South East Asia. You won't find much technology in a Hmong hill village.

The Koryak people, a tribe in Russia, live on the northern part of the Pacific Coast. The land in that area is Arctic tundra, which is very cold. For food, these people catch fish or herd reindeer. Instead of playing computer games or surfing the Internet, Koryak children help hunt and cook food for their family. They also sometimes make their own clothes made of reindeer skin.

Life for these people is much harder than it is for you or me. Could you live comfortably without basic necessities like food, water and electricity?

113

28 Listen and read. Match the tribes 1–3 to the sentences.

a I don't think they need fridges in winter because the average temperature is -25 degrees Celsius!

b You can't have a mobile phone or a computer without electricity!

c How often do they build new homes? Does anyone know?

d I speak some Chinese. I'd like to learn an unusual language.

e In my opinion, it's important to look after your traditions.

f I'm happy I don't have to hunt for my food!

g Their clothes are warmer than ours!

h I enjoy travel, perhaps they like to move.

29 Choose one of the tribes from the text. Imagine you go to live with them for a week. Write a diary entry about a typical day. Think about life without water, food, electricity and technology. Describe your experience.

THINK BIG Do you know of any other groups of people who live without using technology?
Would you like to live without technology? Why/Why not?

30 **Read. Then choose the sentences where speech marks are used correctly.**

Speech marks (" ") come in pairs. You put them around the words that people say.

"I had a great time at my grandpa's house," said Jaime.

Commas, full stops, question marks and exclamation marks usually go inside speech marks at the end of what a person says. Commas go outside speech marks if they come before what somebody says.

1 "I used to ride my bike to school, said Maria."

2 "Did they watch TV in the 1930s?" he asked.

3 Miguel yelled, "I got a new mobile phone!"

4 Karen said", I listened to the radio last night".

31 **Read and match. Make sentences.**

1 Tim asked,

2 "My dad used to travel by bus to school,"

3 Claire yelled,

4 Grandpa said,

a "I used to get water from a pump when I was young."

b "How did people use to cook food?"

c Bahar said.

d "I got a new mp3 player yesterday!"

32 **Rewrite the sentences using speech marks in your notebook.**

1 I just saw a movie about Henry Ford and the Model T, he said.

2 What should we do this weekend? she asked.

3 Do your homework before watching TV! his mother told him.

4 Taylor said, I got a new computer.

5 You need to finish your book report by Friday, said Mr Clark.

6 Happy birthday, Grandma Rose! everyone yelled.

33 **Write sentences using speech marks in your notebook.**

115

34 **Listen, read and repeat.**

1 ge

2 dge

 116

35 **Listen and find. Then say.**

page

fridge

 117

36 **Listen and blend the sounds.**

1 b-a-dge   badge   2 e-dge   edge
3 a-ge   age   4 s-p-o-n-ge sponge
5 b-r-i-dge bridge   6 h-e-dge   hedge
7 c-a-ge   cage   8 l-ar-ge   large

 118

37 **Read aloud. Then listen and chant.**

There's a large fridge
On the bridge.
There's a large page
In the cage.

120

38 Listen and read. In your notebook, write the steps in order.

Gather Information

Review and Learn

Use the Best Idea

Solving a Problem!

Develop Ideas

Define the Problem

39 Talk about what you can do to solve problems in your classroom.

Our class needs a new computer.

I agree. How can we raise enough money to buy one?

PROJECT

40 Make a Problem-Solving worksheet. Work as a group and use the worksheet to solve this problem.

Steps	Details
1 Define the problem	Our class needs to raise money for a new computer.
2 Gather information	
3 Develop ideas	
4 Use the best idea	
5 Review and learn	

41 **Complete the dialogue.**

> feeling playing sleeping was were

A: I ? studying all evening yesterday.

B: Really? Have you got a test today?

A: No. I was ? all day, so I had to stay up late to finish my homework.

B: ? you studying History?

A: Mostly, yes. I didn't have any Maths homework.

B: Were you ? sleepy? What time did you stop?

A: It was very late. My parents were ? .

42 **Work with a partner. Say the differences between the two pictures.**

LONG AGO

> A long time ago, people used to wash their clothes by hand.

NOW

> Now, many people use washing machines to wash their clothes.

I Can

- talk about the past and the present.
- talk about what people used to do.
- calculate average speed.
- use speech marks correctly.

How Well Do I Know It? Can I Use It?

1 Think about it. Read and draw. Practise.

😊 I know this.   😐 I need more practice.   🙁 I don't know this.

1	**Health problems:** allergies, cough, cut…	**PAGES** 58	😊 😐 🙁
2	**Remedies:** drink some juice, get some rest, take some medicine, see a dentist…	59, 62–63	😊 😐 🙁
3	**Endangered animals:** angler fish, chimpanzee, Komodo dragon, tarsier…	74–81	😊 😐 🙁
4	**Activities:** travel by car/travelled by horse and carriage, have electric lights / had oil lamps…	90–91	😊 😐 🙁
5	You **should/shouldn't** stay in bed. They take good care of **themselves**.	62–63	😊 😐 🙁
6	What **should I** do? You **could** call Katie. Or you **could** ask Mum.	66–67	😊 😐 🙁
7	**How many** chimpanzees were there 100 years ago? There **were** more than one million.	78	😊 😐 🙁
8	**Why** are Andean flamingos endangered? They're endangered **because** people are destroying their habitat.	79	😊 😐 🙁
9	We were in a jeep, **so** we **could** go quite close. **Who** are they? **What** could you see? …	82–83	😊 😐 🙁
10	**Did** people **have** mp3 players in 1950? No, they **didn't**. They **listened** to the radio. Before computers, people **used to** write letters.	94–95	😊 😐 🙁
11	What **were you doing** at eleven o'clock? I **was swimming**.	98–99	😊 😐 🙁

121

2 **Get ready.**

A Complete the dialogue. Use the phrases in the box. Then listen and check.

could do
did they do
didn't use to watch
should go out
should watch
used to go out
were watching it

Mum: What's wrong, Kevin?

Kevin: My eyes are sore.

Mum: I know why. You watch too much TV! Look at the time! You ¹ ? two hours ago and you're still here! You ² ? and get some exercise.

Kevin: Oh, Mum!

Mum: Kevin, I'm right. You spend too much time using technology – watching TV and using your mobile phone.

Kevin: So... ?

Mum: Well, that's why your eyes are sore. You ³ ? TV for only one hour a day.

Kevin: Only one hour? How can I do that?

Mum: It's easy. A long time ago, children ⁴ ? TV all the time.

Kevin: What ⁵ ? ?

Mum: They ⁶ ? and play. You ⁷ ? the same!

Kevin: Oh, OK, Mum. Maybe you're right.

B Practise the dialogue in **A** with a partner.

C Ask and answer the questions with a partner.

1 What do you think of Kevin's mum's advice?

2 Do you think you should watch less TV? Why/Why not?

3 What should people do to stay healthy?

Get set.

 STEP 1 Cut out the cards on page 159 of your Activity Book.

 STEP 2 Put the cards face down in two piles: green cards and orange cards. Now you're ready to **Go!**

 Go!

A Read the dialogues.

Dialogue A	Dialogue B
A: What's wrong?	**A:** What's wrong?
B: I've got stomachache.	**B:** I've got stomachache.
A: Why?	**A:** Why?
B: I watched too much TV.	**B:** I ate too many sweets.
A: That doesn't make sense.	**A:** You should go to the school nurse.

B Now play the game. Pick one green card and one orange card. Use them to make a dialogue with a partner. Does the dialogue make sense? If not, pick another orange card. Keep picking orange cards until your dialogue makes sense. Use the card to give advice to your partner. Then change roles and play again.

You should go to the school nurse.

C Act out one of the dialogues for your class.

5 **Write about yourself in your notebook.**

- Do you take care of yourself? Explain.

- What kinds of technology have you got? Did people have this technology 100 years ago? If not, what did they use instead?

- What endangered animals do you know about? Why are they endangered? What could we do to help them?

- What were you learning in English last week? Do you know it now?

All About Me

Date:_____

_____

_____

How Well Do I Know It Now?

6 A **Look at page 106 and your notebook. Draw again.**

B **Use a different colour.**

C **Read and think.**

I can start the next unit.

I can ask my teacher for help and then start the next unit.

I can practise and then start the next unit.

7 **Rate this Checkpoint.**

☆ very easy   ☆ easy   ☆ hard   ☆ very hard   ☆ fun   ☆ OK   ☆ not fun

1
2
3
4
5
6
7
8
9

Units 4–6 Exam Preparation

– Part A –

Look at the pictures. What did Fred do last week? Listen and draw a line from the day to the correct picture. There is one example.

Monday

Tuesday

Wednesday

Thursday

Friday

Saturday

Sunday

– Part B –

Look at the pictures and read the story. Write some words to complete the sentences about the story. You can use 1, 2 or 3 words.

At the dentist's

My name is Vicki. Last Thursday, my younger brother John wasn't very well. When he got home from school, he had a terrible toothache. Mum called the dentist and we went to see him. The dentist is Dad's friend. His name is Mr Jones and he's got curly black hair and red glasses. He's funny. Mr Jones asked John some questions: "How often do you brush your teeth, John?" John said, "I used to brush my teeth twice a day. I don't always brush them in the morning now."

Then John had to sit in the chair and the dentist looked in his mouth. He asked John, "Do you like sweets?" John eats a lot of sweets. The dentist laughed and said, "You shouldn't eat so many sweets. Now, I want you to brush your teeth after every meal – breakfast, lunch and dinner. OK?" We drove home in our car and when we got home, John said, "Can I brush my teeth now? Mum and I laughed."

Examples

John is ___*younger*___ than Vicki.

John went to the dentist last ___*Thursday*___ .

1 John went to the dentist because he had a _____ .

2 Mr Jones is Dad's _____ .

3 John used to brush his teeth _____ .

4 John eats _____ sweets.

5 The dentist told him to brush his teeth after _____ meal.

6 They travelled home by _____ .

Unit 7 Special Days

1 Listen, look and say.

1 Father's Day

2 my parents' anniversary

3 New Year's Eve/Day

4 School Sports Day

5 Midsummer's Day

6 Earth Day

2 Listen, find and say.

3 Play a game.

4 Listen and sing. What special day is this Friday?

What Do We Do on Special Days?

This Friday is a special day –
The last day of the year.
We're going to stay up very late.
At midnight we're going to cheer!

Special days are cool. Special days are fun.
Special days bring special treats for everyone!

On the first of January,
We are going to say,
"Happy New Year!" to everyone
Because it's New Year's Day.

Chorus

There are lots of special days
And this one is a treat.
We're going to have parades and fireworks
And delicious food to eat!

Chorus

5 Listen and match the special days to the actions.

a

wear different clothes

b

give/get presents or a card

c

have a party

d

watch a parade

e

watch fireworks

THINK BIG What other special days can you name?
What other things do you do on special days?

6 **Listen and read. Why is Sam making a cake?**

The Anniversary Party

What are you doing, Sam?

Well, tomorrow is 10th June. I'm making a cake for your anniversary!

1 Sam's parents' anniversary is on the 10th.

Oh! That's nice!

Don't worry. I'm going to take care of everything.

2 Sam wants to help his parents celebrate their wedding anniversary.

We're going to have dinner at Antonio's, your favourite restaurant.

Oh... yes, right!

3 Sam and his family are going to eat out.

Sam, when are we going to have dinner at Antonio's?

Tomorrow night! And then we're all going to come back here to have cake.

4 Sam is planning a little party after the dinner. He's going to give them a card!

5 | Sam's parents like the plans but there's a little problem.

6 | Sam got the date right but the month wrong!

7 **Read and say True or False.**

1 In the story, the next day is 10th June.

2 Sam is making a cake for his parents' birthday.

3 They are all going to have dinner at a restaurant.

4 Sam is right about the day but wrong about the month.

5 Sam's parents' anniversary is on 10th June.

THINK BIG
How do you think Sam feels at the end of the story?
Have you ever made a mistake about the date?
When? What happened?
What other special occasions do people celebrate?

Language in Action

8 Listen and look at the sentences. Help Sam and Christina make more.

watch fireworks   wear special clothes

New Year's Eve/Day   Father's Day   Sports' Day

When   are you going to   watch a parade   ?

We   're going to   watch a parade

on New Year's Day.   .

Is he going to   give presents   ?

Yes, he is   .

9 Read and complete. Change the words in blue.
Then role play with a partner.

Calvin: When are we **go/going** to go to
Grandma's house for their anniversary?

Mum: 10ᵗʰ May.

Calvin: This Saturday? **Are/Is** we going to
have/having a party?

Mum: Yes. Dad's **going to/going** make some
special food and I'm going to bake
a cake.

Calvin: Cool. **I'm going/I go** to make a card
then.

Mum: Good idea!

10 Work with a partner. Act out some of the things you do on special days.
Ask your partner to guess.

11 **Read and say. Now look at the calendar and test your partner.**

> We write: 1st April
>
> We say: On the first of April

January

1st first	2nd second	3rd third	4th fourth
5th fifth	6th sixth	7th seventh	8th eighth
9th ninth	10th tenth	11th eleventh	12th twelfth
13th thirteenth	14th fourteenth	15th fifteenth	16th sixteenth
17th seventeenth	18th eighteenth	19th nineteenth	20th twentieth
21st twenty-first	30th thirtieth	31st thirty-first	

12 **Complete the sentences with true answers.**

1 Today is the ? .
2 Tomorrow is the ? .
3 Yesterday was the ? .
4 Next Monday is the ? .

132

13 **Listen and choose.**

1 4th/14th   2 12th/20th

3 31st/30th   4 2nd/20th

5 1st/21st   6 3rd/4th

14 **Work with a partner and talk about people you are going to visit.**

> Are you going to visit your grandma on the ninth?

> No, I'm going to visit my grandma on the tenth.

15 Read the questions. Think and answer. Collect information as a class.

1 What are some important festivals in your country?

2 When are they?

3 How do people celebrate them?

134
16 Listen and read. Match the titles – to paragraphs – .

> **CONTENT WORDS**
> attraction   celebrate   feast   fight   glacier
> powder   take place   torch   unusual

a The Colour Red

b Dancing on Ice

c The Start of a New Season

d Strange Dinner Guests

Unusual Festivals

Every country has its own festivals to celebrate different things. Some festivals are more interesting than others because they're unusual – and a lot more fun! Here are just a few unusual festivals from around the world.

1 Holi, the festival of colours, takes place every year in India, Nepal and other parts of the world. Holi celebrates the end of winter and the arrival of spring and it lasts for many days. It's also a celebration of good over evil. During the festival, people throw coloured powder and water at each other. Shops and offices close and the streets fill with excited crowds. It's one of the most colourful festivals in the world!

2 The only colour during another famous festival is red. "La Tomatina" takes place in Buñol, Spain, in August. People come from all over the world for a big food fight. La Tomatina, you see, is the festival of throwing tomatoes! All over the city, people run through the streets throwing red tomatoes at each other. The streets get very messy but everyone has a good time.

3 Another strange and cold festival takes place every May or June in Peru. At Quyllur Rit'i, or the Festival of the Snow Star, people celebrate with music and dancing on top of a glacier! The festival lasts for three days and, at the end, everyone walks out together carrying torches of fire.

4 Finally, how about a festival with animals? On the last weekend in November, people in Lopburi, Thailand, invite some unusual guests to dinner at the Monkey Buffet Festival. Hundreds of monkeys come to the buffet, where they feast on fruit, nuts and vegetables. It's a great tourist attraction, as people from all over the world come to watch it.

Unusual or not, festivals have one thing in common. They bring people together and they give them a reason to celebrate and have fun.

17 **Look at 16. Read and choose.**

1 Holi is a **short/long** festival.

2 Holi celebrates **different colours/a new season**.

3 La Tomatina takes place in **many towns/a town** in Spain.

4 There are **no tourists/lots of tourists** at the tomato throwing festival.

5 **The food/The guests** are important at the Monkey Buffet.

6 During Quyllur Rit'i people **eat and drink/play music and dance**.

135
18 **Look at some more festivals. What do people do at them? Guess and match. Then listen and check.**

1 The Mud festival (Boryeong, South Korea)

2 The Ice and Snow festival (Harbin, China)

3 The Running of the Bulls festival (Pamplona, Spain)

THINK BIG Which of the festivals on this page would you like to go to? Why?

a Some animals chase people in the streets of the town.

b People have baths and play with something.

c People swim in very cold water.

d People often fall and injure themselves.

e People make beautiful things.

PROJECT

19 **Work in groups. Make your own Unusual Festival fact file. Use the notes for help. Then present it to the class.**

1 What is your festival's name?

2 What is it going to celebrate?

3 Where is it going to take place and when?

4 How long is it?

5 What is going to happen during the festival?

Traditional Foods Festival

Name: Traditional Foods festival
Celebrates: Food from around the world
Where: At school
How long: 2-9 September
During the festival: Prepare and taste traditional foods from around the world

137

20 Listen and read. Why is Nick tired?

Rita and Nick are talking.

Rita: You look tired, Nick. What's up?

Nick: My aunt and her family are coming from Australia today to spend a month with us. On Wednesday, I cleaned my room because I'm going to share it with my cousin. Yesterday, I cut the grass in the garden because we're going to have a barbeque this evening. And today, I helped my grandma in the kitchen because we're preparing a surprise cake!

Rita: Wow! That's a lot of work! Aren't you going to meet them at the airport?

Nick: No way. I'm going to bed. I'm exhausted!

21 Look at 20. Complete the chart.

I cleaned my room. I'm going to share it with my cousin.
I ¹ ⸮ my room ² ⸮ I ³ ⸮ it with my cousin.

22 Read and match.

1 I studied all weekend

2 Beth went to bed early

3 Kemal cooked a lot of food

4 Fred took his umbrella

5 Claudia bought sunscreen

6 I tidied the living room

because

a it's going to rain today.

b my grandma is going to visit us.

c he's having a party this evening.

d we're going to have a History test tomorrow.

e she's going to get up early tomorrow.

f she's going on holiday next week.

23 Look at 22. Hide a–f. Test your partner.

Beth went to bed early because…

…she's going to get up early tomorrow!

24 **Look at 21. Read and complete.**

> buy a new camera   make a cake   not cook
> practise every day   read the whole book   take his trainers

1 We ❓ this morning because we're celebrating Mum's birthday.

2 I ❓ today because I'm going to return it to the library tomorrow.

3 Will ❓ because he's going to play football this afternoon.

4 The girls ❓ because they're taking part in a dance competition.

5 Maria ❓ because she's going to take lots of photos at the Carnival.

6 Mum ❓ because we're going to have dinner at a restaurant.

25 **Read and complete.**

From: alberto@homemail.com
To: selda@europemail.com
Subject: I'm so excited!

Hey Selda,

Remember I told you we're going on holiday around Europe? Well, we're finally ready to leave! Last week, however, was really busy for the whole family. Dad ¹❓ (get) a special driving license last Tuesday because we ²❓ (rent) a car. I ³❓ (buy) new swimming trunks yesterday because we ⁴❓ (spend) a few days at the beach in Greece. And last night, Mum ⁵❓ (pack) her brushes and paints in the suitcase because she ⁶❓ (paint) in Italy.

I have to go now. Watch out for my next email from Spain!

Love,
Alberto

26 **Complete the sentences. Then write them in your notebook.**

1 I got up early today because ❓.

2 ❓ because we're celebrating my grandma's birthday.

3 I cleaned my room because ❓.

4 ❓ because I'm going to a party.

5 I asked Mum for some money ❓.

6 ❓ because we're going away for the weekend.

Leap Years

1   How long is a year? Most people say it's 365 days, since it takes about 365 days for the Earth to travel around the Sun. Well, not exactly – it actually takes 365 days, 5 hours, 49 minutes and 12 seconds. If a calendar has only 365 days, what happens to the extra time? To solve this problem, every four years we add one day to the calendar. February 29th is called a leap day and the year is called a leap year. Other years are common years. There are 366 days in a leap year.

2   Julius Caesar was a Roman Emperor in the 1st century BC. He created leap years to solve the problem of the extra time in the calendar. However, people didn't like the change and Greeks and Romans had lots of superstitions about unlucky things in leap years. They believed it was unlucky to start a new job, start a journey, marry or buy or sell something in a leap year. Some people in Greece still consider it very unlucky to marry in a leap year.

27   **Read the questions. Think and answer. Check with the class.**

1   Do all months have the same number of days?

2   Which is the shortest month?

3   Do all years have the same number of days?

28   **Read the article quickly to find these numbers. What do they mean in the text?**

365   29th   four   366

29   **Look at the years. Which are leap years? Which are common years? How do you know?**

1996

1994

2029

2018

2006

2002

2012

2020

2015

3   This special day, however, is not only connected with bad things. In some parts of the world, such as Ireland, Scotland, Finland and Denmark, the tradition is that women can propose marriage to a man on a leap day. If the man says no, he has to buy the woman a present.

4   How do we know which years are leap years? The main rule is that years that can be divided evenly by four are leap years. 2012 divides by four, so 2016, 2020 and 2024 are also leap years.

5   People born on a leap day are called leapers. If you know a leaper, make sure you say "Happy Birthday", because their actual birthday happens only once every four years! Does this mean that they only grow a year older every four years? What do you think?

138

30   **Listen and read. Complete the sentences. Use words from the text.**

1   A 🔑 year is 365 days long.
2   We add one day to the calendar 🔑 four years.
3   The first leap year was in the 🔑 century BC.
4   There were lots of 🔑 about leap years in ancient Rome and Greece.
5   Some Greek people think it's unlucky to 🔑 in a leap year.
6   To find if a year is a leap year, you should 🔑 it by four.

31   **Let's see what you know about other superstitions. Read and match.**

1   In Japan, having a black   a   cat brings good luck to your house.
2   In China, the number   b   mirror gives you seven years bad luck.
3   The number 7 is   c   lucky all around the world.
4   In the USA, breaking a   d   4 sounds like death, so it's unlucky.

32   **In your notebook, write three sentences about superstitions in your country.**

THINK **When is the next leap year?**
BIG   **Are there lucky or unlucky days in your country?**

33 **Read. Then match the parts of the email.**

closing and signature   friend's email address   greeting
main body of the email   what your email is about
your email address

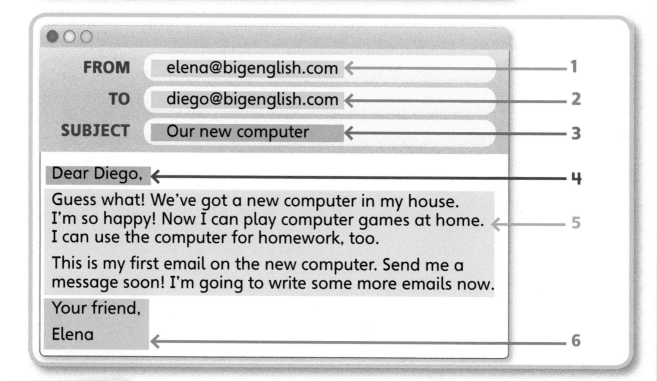

FROM   elena@bigenglish.com ← ——————— 1

TO   diego@bigenglish.com ← ——————— 2

SUBJECT   Our new computer ← ——————— 3

Dear Diego, ← ——————————————— 4

Guess what! We've got a new computer in my house.
I'm so happy! Now I can play computer games at home. ← 5
I can use the computer for homework, too.

This is my first email on the new computer. Send me a
message soon! I'm going to write some more emails now.

Your friend,

Elena ← ——————————————— 6

Writing Steps

34 **Write an email.**

1 Think who you're going to write to.
2 Write the two email addresses.
3 Think about what you're going to write about.
4 Write a subject for your email and your greeting.
5 Think of what you want to write in the email.
6 Write two paragraphs for the body of the email.
7 Write the closing and signature.
8 Read your email and check for mistakes.
Now send!

140
35 **Listen, read and repeat.**

1 ue   **2** u_e   **3** ure

141
36 **Listen and find. Then say.**

 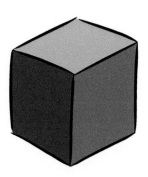 

blue   **cu**be   **trea**sure

142
37 **Listen and blend the sounds.**

1 g-l-ue   glue   **2** t-r-ue   true
3 c-u-te   cute   **4** p-i-c-t-ure   picture
5 n-a-t-ure nature   **6** d-u-ke   duke
7 h-u-ge   huge   **8** S-ue   Sue

143
38 **Read aloud. Then listen and chant.**

Hi, Sue
Is it true?
It's so cute, it's so blue,
It's really huge!
Is that a monster
In the picture?

39 Write a definition for the word tradition.

 40 Listen and look. Number the traditions in order.

145

?   ?   ?   ?

41 Talk about some of your family traditions.

Does your family have a special tradition for New Year's Eve?

Yes. We always eat noodles on New Year's Eve!

PROJECT

 42 Make a Traditions Around the World poster. Display your posters in the corridors at school.

children's day

costumes

carp kites

origami

rice cakes

JAPAN

Complete the dialogue.

Mum:	Hi, Mike. Why do you look so tired?
Mike:	We ¹ 🔲 a party because tomorrow is Father's Day.
Mum:	Oh, right. Did you clean the house?
Mike:	No, but we ² 🔲 all the food because tomorrow we ³ 🔲 buy the presents.
Mum:	Is everything ready now?
Mike:	Yes! We ⁴ 🔲 garden decorations because the weather ⁵ 🔲 be sunny, so the party is going ⁶ 🔲 outside.
Mum:	That sounds great!

> are going to   cooked
> is going to   made
> organised   to be

 Research and answer the questions about a festival in another country.

1 When do people celebrate this day?

2 What do people do on this day?

 Play the Holiday Plans game.

> On New Year's Day, I'm going to watch a parade.

> On New Year's Day, Alicia is going to watch a parade and I'm going to sleep until midday.

> On New Year's Day, Alicia is going to watch a parade, Robert is going to sleep late and I'm going to visit my grandparents.

I Can

- talk about special days and dates.
- talk about the past and the future.
- talk about world festivals.
- write an email.

Unit 8 Hobbies

1 Listen, look and say.

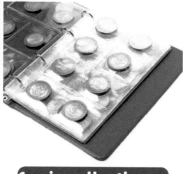
1 coin collection

2 doll collection

3 shell collection

4 toy car collection

5 basketball

6 chess

7 music

8 video games

2 Listen, find and say.

3 Play a game.

4 Listen and sing. Who is a terrible singer?

The Best and the Worst

Matthew collects toy cars.
He's got one hundred and seven.
But Pam's car collection is bigger.
She's got three hundred
And eleven!

Kay is good at games.
She's really good at chess.
But Paul is even better than Kay.
And Liz, well, she's the best!

**What's your hobby, Bobby?
What do you like doing?
What's your hobby, Bobby?
What is fun for you?**

Steve is a terrible singer.
Emma's worse than Steve.
But David's singing is the worst.
When he sings, people leave!

It's good to have a hobby.
Some people have got a few.
Even if you're not the best,
It still is fun to do!

Chorus

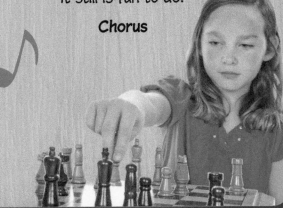

150

5 Listen and answer. What hobbies do they enjoy?

1  **Freddie**
2  **Sylvia**
3  **Philip**
4  **Kayla**

Freddie has got a big toy car collection.

THINK BIG Which child in 5 is the most like you? Why?
What other things can you collect?

song/vocabulary Unit 8 **129**

6 **Listen and read. What part is Christina going to have?**

1 Christina's dad is excited about this year's school play.

2 He wants Christina to be a star.

3 Snow White is the most important character in the play.

4 The Evil Queen is another important character in the play.

5 There aren't many other female characters in the play.

6 Christina is taller than her friends so she's going to play a tree. It's a small part but Dad is still proud.

7 **Read and say the name: Ruth, Lizzie, Christina or Snow White.**

1 She's the most important character in the play.

2 She's the tallest girl in the class.

3 She's the best actor in the class.

4 She's a better singer than Christina.

5 She's going to be the best tree in the class.

THINK BIG Have you ever acted in a school play? Did you enjoy it? Why/Why not?
Why is Christina's dad proud of her at the end of the story?

Language in Action

8 Listen and look at the sentences. Help Sam and Christina make more.

singer   dancer   basketball player

Laura is a   good   chess player   .

Yoko is a   better   chess player   than   Laura   .

Alex is   the best   chess player   in the class   .

My singing is   bad   .

Her singing is   worse than   mine   .

Claire is   the worst   singer   of all   .

9 Use the adjectives to complete the sentences.

1 John's 🔑 artist in our school. (good)

2 She's 🔑 girl in our class. (short)

3 Julie's 🔑 football player in her team. (tall)

4 I've got 🔑 hair in my family. (long)

5 My sister's got 🔑 hair in her class. (curly)

6 Ahmad is 🔑 friend I've got. (funny)

10 Think of people in your family. Talk about the things they can do.

My dad is a good singer.
My sister is the best chess
player in the family.

11 **Read. Then complete the dialogue.**

> I'm good at video games.
> He's good at music.
> She's bad at chess.
> They're bad at basketball.

A: What are you good ¹ 🔲 , Sally?

B: Umm. I love playing the guitar. I think I'm ² 🔲 at music.

A: You definitely are. What are you ³ 🔲 at?

B: I'm pretty ⁴ 🔲 basketball but I am OK at football.

12 **Look at the pictures. Complete the dialogues.**

> bad   better   good   than (x2)   the best   the worst   worse

1

A: Sam is a 🔲 singer.

B: Yes. But Mike is 🔲 Sam.

A: Yes. But Terry is 🔲 singer of all.
He really can't sing!

2

A: Vincent is a 🔲 actor.

B: Yes. But Tim is 🔲 Vincent.

A: True! But Louisa is 🔲 in our class.

13 **Work with a partner and find out more about people in your class.
Report your findings to the class.**

14 What do you do after school? Have you got a hobby? Make a list of hobbies as a class.

155

15 Listen and read. Match topics a–f to paragraphs 1–6.

> **CONTENT WORDS**
> creativity croquet embroidery employers handmade
> imagination insect needle net sewing spare time thread

a Children's toys

b Making things

c Collecting as a hobby

d Women and sports

e Modern hobbies

f How hobbies are good for people

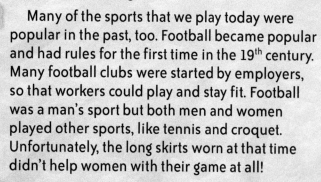

Hobbies in the Past

1 Like fashion, hobbies change with the times. In our days, a lot of hobbies use technology: we take digital photos and post them online and children play computer games. But what did people use to do before this technology? Let's take a look at some hobbies that were popular more than 100 years ago.

2 Many of the sports that we play today were popular in the past, too. Football became popular and had rules for the first time in the 19th century. Many football clubs were started by employers, so that workers could play and stay fit. Football was a man's sport but both men and women played other sports, like tennis and croquet. Unfortunately, the long skirts worn at that time didn't help women with their game at all!

3 Many women and girls spent their spare time doing sewing and embroidery. They used a needle and thread to make tiny stitches on a piece of fabric. They made clothes and accessories such as scarves and gloves. They also made home decorations. They created beautiful pictures of flowers, birds and other patterns. They also used to embroider cushions, tablecloths and rugs.

4 Girls in the 19th century used to play with dolls and dolls' houses. At that time, toys were handmade. The dolls' heads were often made of china and the bodies were made of wood or calico. Rocking horses were also very popular. They were made of wood and their tails were made of real horsehair. Boys used to play with toy trains and railways.

5 Finally, people in the 19th century loved nature, so one popular hobby was collecting and drawing butterflies. People used to catch butterflies in nets and fix them on special boards with pins. They used to draw pictures that showed all the details and colours of the beautiful insects.

6 Past or present, hobbies are a great way to pass the time. They help us show our creativity and use our imagination.

16 **Look at 15. Correct and make true sentences.**

In the 19th century,

1 children used to play computer games.

3 only men played tennis.

5 dolls were made of plastic.

2 football didn't have rules.

4 women and girls used to make toys.

6 people used to take photos of butterflies.

THINK BIG Were the hobbies in the article ever popular in your country? Are they popular now? Which hobby would you like to try?

17 **Look at the hobbies. Match to the jobs in the box.**

1 playing sports

3 reading/writing

5 making clothes

7 using computers

9 music

2 cooking/food

4 films

6 traveling

8 drawing/painting

10 collecting old things

animator   cookbook writer
DJ   fashion designer
film director
fitness instructor
flight attendant
museum guide
newspaper editor
special FX artist

18 **Look at 17. Ask and answer with a partner. Add more ideas.**

What are your hobbies?

What are you good at?

You could be a music journalist!

I love music.

I know everything about my favourite artists. I can answer any question.

PROJECT

19 **Write an entry for a Careers Advice leaflet. Then present it to the class.**

Your hobby is:	sports	
You're good at:	playing a sport	You could be an athlete.
	watching sports	You could be a sports journalist.
	teaching people	You could be a fitness instructor.

157

20 **Listen and read. What does Trish collect?**

Trish and Kevin are in the kitchen. Trish is making a sandwich.

Kevin: Have you got a hobby, Trish?

Trish: Yes! I collect photos of unusual things. Wait. Let me get my iPad and I'll show you.

Kevin: Wow! These are great. Do you take the photos yourself?

Trish: Some of them. The most interesting photos are from the Internet. The vegetables are the strangest. Look, that potato looks like a heart!

Kevin: Oh, yes! Ha ha! But these carrot fingers are funnier! And it's a better photo than the potato.

Trish: Yes, you're right. Oh! And look at this tomato I'm cutting! Quick! Where's my camera?

21 **Look at 20. Complete the chart.**

funny strange	These carrot fingers are ¹ ?. Your photos are **better than** mine.	The vegetables are ³ ?. This is **the best**.
a good photo interesting photos	It's ² ? the potato. You've got **nicer photos than** me.	⁴ ? photos are from the Internet. This is **the nicest photo**.

22 **Copy the chart and complete.**

1 boring	more boring	¹ ?
2 intelligent	² ?	³ ?
3 tall	⁴ ?	the tallest
4 easy	⁵ ?	⁶ ?
5 organised	⁷ ?	⁸ ?

23 **Read and complete. Use more, the most and than.**

There are lots of hobbies to choose from. Some are more enjoyable ¹ 🔑 others but there are also some very boring ones. What's ² 🔑 boring hobby in the world? I think watching trains is ³ 🔑 boring ⁴ 🔑 collecting stamps but some people love both!

I think skydiving is ⁵ 🔑 interesting hobby. People think it's dangerous but it isn't ⁶ 🔑 dangerous ⁷ 🔑 driving. There are more car accidents ⁸ 🔑 skydiving accidents!

24 **Look at the chart. Play a game.**

	Juan	Erol	Steven
funny	★★★	★	★★★★★★
organised	★★★★★★	★★	★★★
fit	★★★	★★★★★★	★★
a good singer	★★★	★★	★★★★★★
a creative artist	★★★★★★	★	★★★

Erol is funnier than Steven.

True!

False! Steven is the best singer.

25 **Make the questions. Ask and answer. Then write in your notebook.**

IN YOUR FAMILY...

1. Who is/old person?
2. Are you/young?
3. What's/popular TV programme?
4. Who's/creative?
5. Are you/organised/your dad?
6. Are you/a good cook/your mum?

Who's the oldest person in your family?

My great-grandpa. He's 98!

The World's Weirdest Collections

1   Think of museums and you might think of history, dust and very old things. However, some museums are famous not for old things but for their unusual collections. Read on to find out about three weird museums around the world.

2   In Avanos, Turkey, you can find a hair museum! It all started when a potter from Avanos was saying goodbye to a friend who was leaving the town. This friend gave the potter a lock of her hair and he put it in his shop. When other people asked about it, he told them the story. Many people wanted to leave a lock of their own hair behind, too, so the museum was born! Now there are thousands of different locks of hair in the museum. Twice a year, the potter invites people with the most beautiful hair to come back and have pottery lessons for free!

26   Read the questions. Think and answer. Collect information with the class.

1   What are some museums in your city or country?
2   Do you like visiting museums? Why/Why not?
3   Do you think museums are important? Why/Why not?

27   Read the article quickly and complete.

Name of museum	Where is it?	What can you see there?
Avanos Hair Museum	1	2
3	4	5
6	7	Information about UFO sightings

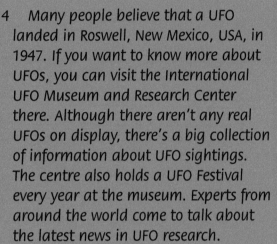

3 The only way you can reach another interesting museum is underwater, so visitors have to be good at snorkelling! The Museum of Underwater Art, inside the National Marine Park of the Yucatán Peninsula of Mexico, displays a large number of sculptures. Some of the sculptures were made by British artist Jason deCaires Taylor. The artist wanted his art to be part of life under the sea. Plants, corals and other marine life make his sculptures their home, and so they become part of the artwork.

4 Many people believe that a UFO landed in Roswell, New Mexico, USA, in 1947. If you want to know more about UFOs, you can visit the International UFO Museum and Research Center there. Although there aren't any real UFOs on display, there's a big collection of information about UFO sightings. The centre also holds a UFO Festival every year at the museum. Experts from around the world come to talk about the latest news in UFO research.

158

28 **Listen and read. Then choose the correct answers.**

1 The Hair Museum displays hair from **the potter/different people**.

2 The potter's friend **gave the potter some hair/told the potter an interesting story**.

3 People must **walk a long way/swim** to visit the Museum of Underwater Art.

4 Plants, corals and marine life **live in the sculptures/make sculptures** under the sea.

5 At the UFO Museum you can **see a real UFO/learn a lot about UFOs**.

6 There is a **UFO sighting/UFO festival** every year.

29 **Can you imagine a different kind of unusual museum? Create a fact file. Answer: What? Where? Why?**

THINK BIG **Which museum would you like to visit? One of the three museums in the article or the one in your fact file? Why?**

30 Read. Then match the parts of the informal letter.

> address   body of informal letter   closing and signature   date   greeting

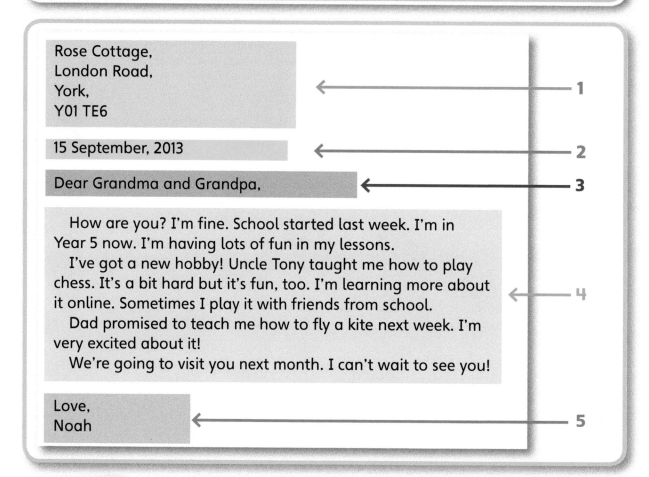

Rose Cottage,
London Road,
York,
Y01 TE6 ← 1

15 September, 2013 ← 2

Dear Grandma and Grandpa, ← 3

   How are you? I'm fine. School started last week. I'm in Year 5 now. I'm having lots of fun in my lessons.
   I've got a new hobby! Uncle Tony taught me how to play chess. It's a bit hard but it's fun, too. I'm learning more about it online. Sometimes I play it with friends from school.
   Dad promised to teach me how to fly a kite next week. I'm very excited about it!
   We're going to visit you next month. I can't wait to see you! ← 4

Love,
Noah ← 5

Writing Steps

31 **Write an informal letter to a friend or family member.**

1 Write your address.
2 Write the date.
3 Think of a person to write to.
4 Choose a hobby to write about.
5 Think of what you want to tell him/her.
6 Start with a greeting.
7 Write the body of your letter.
8 Finish with the closing and signature.

160
32 **Listen, read and repeat.**

1 y

2 igh

161
33 **Listen and find. Then say.**

fly

high

162
34 **Listen and blend the sounds.**

1 s-k-y	sky	**2** t-r-y	try
3 m-y	my	**4** l-igh-t	light
5 f-igh-t	fight	**6** b-y	by
7 n-igh-t	night	**8** r-igh-t	right

163
35 **Read aloud. Then listen and chant.**

Let's fly, let's fight.
Let's try
And light the sky
At night!

Values | Be a good sport.

36 Listen and look. Decide which children are good sports and which are bad sports.

1

2

3

4

37 Role play with a partner.

You won! It was a good game.

You played well, too.

PROJECT

38 Make a paper bag puppet. Use the puppets to role play scenes in which they're good sports.

39 **Look and complete the sentences.**

1 Mark is a 🔲 dancer than Kelly.

2 Sharon is a 🔲 dancer than Mark.

3 Sharon is 🔲 dancer in the group.

4 Mark is 🔲 dancer of the three students.

40 **Complete the sentences.**

1 Terrence's shell collection is 🔲 in the class. (boring)

2 Fatih is 🔲 person in our class. (organised)

3 The dolls in Sandy's collection are 🔲 than my dolls. (interesting)

4 I've got a lot of cartoons in my collection but this one is 🔲. (funny)

41 **Complete with information about yourself. Find out about your partner. Then report to the class.**

1 I am good at... . ...is a better... than I am.

2 I am not good at... . ...is a worse... than I am.

I Can

- talk about people's hobbies.
- make comparisons.
- talk about hobbies in the past.
- write an informal letter.

Unit 9

Learning New Things

 166

1 **Listen, look and say.**

1 dance like a hip-hop artist

2 sing like a rock star

3 bake a cake

4 snowboard

5 play the guitar

6 play badminton

你好

7 speak Chinese

8 draw comic books

9 build a robot

10 make a website

 167

2 **Listen, find and say.**

 3 **Play a game.**

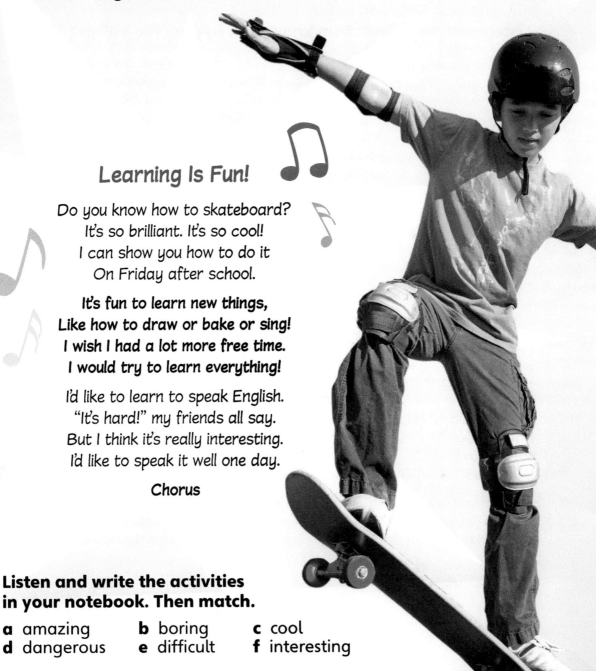

4 Listen and sing. What's brilliant and cool?

Learning Is Fun! ♪

Do you know how to skateboard?
It's so brilliant. It's so cool!
I can show you how to do it
On Friday after school.

It's fun to learn new things,
Like how to draw or bake or sing!
I wish I had a lot more free time.
I would try to learn everything!

I'd like to learn to speak English.
"It's hard!" my friends all say.
But I think it's really interesting.
I'd like to speak it well one day.

Chorus

170

5 Listen and write the activities
in your notebook. Then match.

a amazing   **b** boring   **c** cool
d dangerous **e** difficult **f** interesting

THINK BIG
Which things in **1** can you do?
What do you think of the talents in **1**? Use the words from
5 in your answers.
What skills would you like to learn? Why?

Story

6 **Listen and read. Does Sam know how to play the guitar?**

The Best in the Class

Isn't that boy in your class, Sam?

Oh, yes! That's Jake.

1 Sam and Christina are walking home from school. They see a boy from Sam's class.

Hi, Jake! You're really good at playing the guitar.

Thanks!

2 Sam thinks that Jake can play the guitar very well.

Do you know how to play the guitar?

No, I don't.

3 Sam doesn't know how to play the guitar.

Would you like to learn? I can teach you!

Yes, I'd like to. Thanks!

4 Jake wants to teach Sam how to play the guitar.

5 Sam tries to play the guitar. But he's not very good!

6 Christina thinks Sam's guitar playing is awful.

7 **Correct the sentences. Write the correct sentences in your notebook.**

1 Jake is really good at playing the piano.
2 Sam knows how to play the guitar.
3 Sam wants to teach Jake to play the guitar.
4 Sam is good at playing the guitar.
5 Christina thinks Sam's playing is great.

THINK BIG **What are you good at doing? What do you have to do to learn how to do a new thing well?**

8 Listen and look at the sentences. Help Sam and Christina make more.

draw comic books   make a website

play badminton   dance like a hip-hop artist

Do you know how to   play the piano   ?   Yes, I do   .

Does he know how to   bake a cake   ?   No, he doesn't   .

What would she like to learn how to do   ?

She'd like to learn how to   sing like a rock star   .

They'd like to learn how to   speak Chinese   .

9 Complete the questions and answers.

1 Do you ? the guitar?

? . But I can play the piano.

3 ? sing?

? . They sing very well.

2 Does he ? dance?

? . He dances every weekend.

4 ? draw?

? . She's terrible at art.

10 Look and read. Write the answers in your notebook.

1

What would they like
to learn how to do?

2

What would she like
to learn how to do?

3

What would he like
to learn how to do?

11 **Read. Then complete the sentences.**

What do you think of snowboarding?	I think it's dangerous.
What does she think of baking cakes?	She thinks it's boring.
What do they ¹ 🔑 of learning Chinese?	They ² 🔑 it's difficult.
What does he ³ 🔑 of playing the piano?	He ⁴ 🔑 it's amazing.

12 **Write questions and answers in your notebook.**

1

she/make pizza/?
cool/.

2

he/skateboard/?
fun/.

3

they/build a
robot/?
difficult/.

4

you/watch tennis/?
interesting/.

13 **Ask and answer with a partner.**

What do you think
of hip-hop dancing?

I think it's
amazing.

14 How many different body parts can you name? Make a list as a class.

175

15 Listen and read. Which three main body parts are mentioned?

CONTENT WORDS

bone brain contract flexible joint motion muscle
nerves organs precision relax skeleton support

Our Amazing Bodies

1 There are many things that we enjoy doing: playing sports and musical instruments, going for a walk or a run, cycling and doing crafts. The list is endless. We use our body for all these things but we hardly ever think about how it works.

2 Our bodies are like an amazing machine. Different parts work together to make everything move with precision. The most important body parts that help us move are our bones, muscles and joints. These three things make up our musculoskeletal system. Without this system, we wouldn't be able to stand, walk or move in any way.

3 Our bones are our body's frame. They make up our skeleton. Our bones protect and support the organs within our body and give it shape. Without bones, our body would look like an octopus! There are more bones in the body parts that need to do finer movements. That's why there are twenty-seven different bones in each hand.

4 Our joints connect two or more bones to each other. Our knees, elbows and shoulders are all joints. Joints are important because they allow us to be flexible. Without working joints, our body wouldn't be able to move.

5 Our muscles are also important for motion. Muscles are strong and flexible. They pull bones in different directions. By doing so, they help our body move: they contract (become shorter) or relax (become longer) according to the movement we need.

6 Of course, our muscles, bones and joints don't move by themselves. Our brain and nerves help out. For example, if we want to kick a football, our brain needs to tell our nerves that we want to move our foot. Our nerves send a message to our muscles. Our muscles get shorter and, by doing that, they lift our leg. As a result, we can kick the ball.

7 So, next time you are rushing to get to a lesson, remember how amazing it is that your body gets you there at all!

16 Look at **15**. Read and choose.

1 Bones, muscles and joints make up our **skeleton/musculoskeletal system**.

2 Without our **organs/bones**, our body wouldn't have any shape.

3 Our joints connect two or more **bones/muscles** together.

4 There are twenty-seven bones in our **body/hand**.

5 Our muscles contract and **relax/kick** to move our body.

6 When we want to move, our muscles take messages from our **nerves/joints**.

17 176 Guess and match the amazing body facts. Then listen and check.

		a	They work twenty-four hours a day.
1	Our bones	**b**	It's got eight muscles in it.
2	Our brain	**c**	They're small but very strong.
3	Our heart muscles	**d**	They've got holes in them, like a sponge.
4	Our tongue	**e**	It uses electricity, just like a computer.
		f	It uses about 20% of the oxygen in our body.

18 Look at **17**. Discuss with a partner. Add more facts from the article.

It's got eight muscles and it's very strong. What is it?

I think it's...

THINK BIG Look back at the list of body words from **14**. What do the things in the list do?

PROJECT

19 Make an **Amazing Body** poster. Then present it to the class.

1 Find or draw a body picture.

2 Add amazing body facts.

3 Put your poster on the wall. Which facts did your friends find?

Skin

Our skin is our body's biggest organ. It protects us from germs. Without it, we would get ill more often.

20 Listen and read. Why is Martin very helpful today?

Martin's mum is back from the supermarket.

Mum: Hi, honey! Oh, these bags are heavy!

Martin: Hi, Mum! I'll take them! And I'll put the shopping away. You just sit down and relax.

Mum: That's very kind. Oh, no! I left my phone in the car.

Martin: I'll get it for you.

Mum: Oh! Thanks. I really haven't got time to rest. I think I'll start cooking now.

Martin: Don't worry, Mum. I'll make dinner tonight!

Mum: Hmm... You're being very helpful, Martin... Is everything OK?

Martin: Sure! I'm helpful because you're the best mum in the world!

Mum: OK, Martin. What do you want?

Martin: Can I go to a rock concert on Saturday? Please?

21 Look at **20**. Complete the chart.

¹ 🔲 put the shopping away. I'll ² 🔲 dinner tonight! I'll take your bags.	I think ³ 🔲 cooking now. I'll have pizza and a cola, please.

22 Read and match. Then make offers and quick decisions.

1 **A:** My camera isn't working.

2 **A:** Would you like to order now?

3 **A:** I'm cold.

4 **A:** Your white shirt is dirty.

5 **A:** You could take a taxi.

6 **A:** This exercise is very difficult.

a **B:** Don't worry. I'll help you.

b **B:** I'll fix it for you!

c **B:** Yes, please. I'll have a salad.

d **B:** OK. I'll wear the blue one.

e **B:** Wait. I'll give you my jacket.

f **B:** No, it's too expensive. I'll take the bus.

23 **Read. Make offers. Use will.**

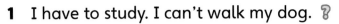

> answer it for you   cook for you   read it for you
> show you   take him out for you   tidy it for you

1 I have to study. I can't walk my dog. 🔖

2 The phone's ringing and I'm very busy. 🔖

3 I've got a new TV and I don't know how to use it. 🔖

4 What's on this menu? I haven't got my glasses. 🔖

5 I'm hungry. 🔖

6 The living room is a mess and I have to go to work. 🔖

24 **Read and complete. Use I think I'll... .**

1 There are two good films on TV – a comedy and an action film.

Mark: 🔖 . I love a good laugh!

2 It's still early. You can walk to school or take the bus.

Mark: 🔖 . I need the exercise.

3 You're at your friend's house. She's offering orange juice or apple juice.

Mark: 🔖 . I don't like orange juice.

4 You've got two exams and only half an hour to study: History or Geography?

Mark: 🔖 . I'm good at Geography, anyway.

25 **Look at 23. Discuss with a partner. Add your ideas.**

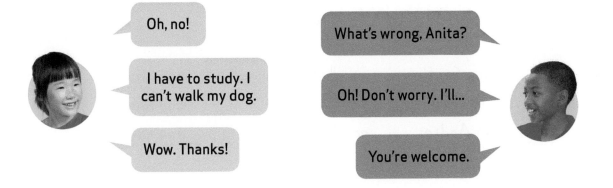

Extraordinary Kids

1   Learning how to do something takes time and effort. Some of us are fast learners, some are average and some take things slowly. But there are some children in the world who are born with extraordinary talents. They learn much faster and can do things better than professional adults!

2   Gregory Smith was born in 1990 in Keswick, Virginia, in the United States. He could read before he was two years old. At ten, he went to university. By sixteen, Gregory had several university degrees, including a Maths degree. But he's more than just a genius. He travels the world trying to help young people. He hopes that he can help make the world a safer and more peaceful place for everyone.

 Look at the talents. Who's good at them in your class? When did they start?

> dance   do Sudoku   draw   gymnastics   play an instrument
> play chess   solve Maths problems   speak another language

Who's good at gymnastics?

Me! I started when I was six. I go to gym lessons every week. I love it!

 Read the article quickly and complete.

Gregory Smith:	good at: studying	age now: [1] ?
Yuto Miyazawa:	good at: [2] ?	age now: [3] ?
Aelita Andre:	good at: [4] ?	age now: [5] ?

3   At just eight years old, Yuto Miyazawa was already a professional musician! Born in 2000, Yuto started having guitar lessons when he was four years old. Soon, everyone knew he had an extraordinary talent for music. Yuto has performed with music legends Ozzy Osbourne, Les Paul and G. E. Smith and has appeared on several TV talk shows. At the age of twelve, he joined "The Robotix", a rock band of young musicians, as the lead guitarist. Journalists have described him as "The Mozart of Metal".

4   People in Australia are talking about another amazing young artist. Aelita Andre started showing her paintings soon after her second birthday. Her father, also an artist, says that Aelita started to paint before she could even walk. In 2011, at the age of four, she had her first solo exhibition in New York. All the paintings sold out in the first two weeks. Some people say that Aelita is too young to be considered a real artist but art collectors are interested in her work and buy her paintings.

5   Not everyone can be a genius but we've all got our own special talents. The important thing is to work hard and not give up!

179

28 **Listen and read. Match the people 1–3 to the facts a–f.**

1 Gregory   **2** Yuto   **3** Aelita

a He/She was a professional musician at the age of eight.

b He/She started showing work before the age of three.

c He/She had several university degrees by the age of sixteen.

d Collectors are interested in his/her work.

e He/She travels a lot.

f He/She has appeared in TV talk shows.

29 **Look at the notes. Choose a person and write a biography in your notebook.**

Nadia Comaneci
Born 1961, Romania
Gymnast
Started doing gymnastics: in kindergarten
Won three Olympic gold medals: when she was fourteen

Akrit Jaswal
Born 1993, India
Doctor
Started operating: age of seven
Goal: to find a cure for cancer

BIG **Do you think it's easy to be a genius? What are the good things and bad things about it?**

30 **Read. Then match the parts of the review.**

> body of review   final sentence   online name and date
> rating   title   topic sentence

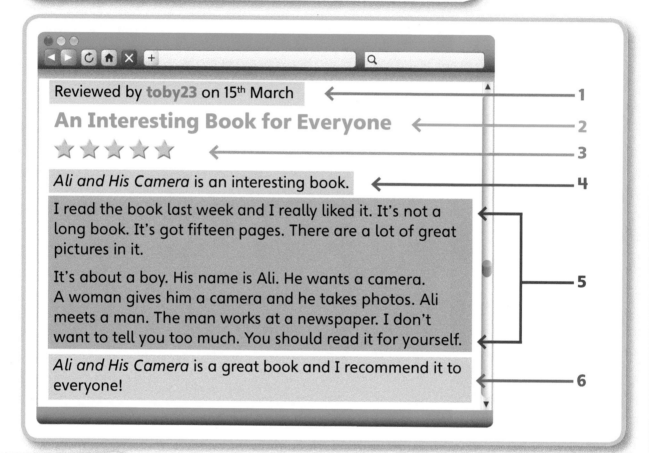

Reviewed by **toby23** on 15th March — 1

An Interesting Book for Everyone — 2

★ ★ ★ ★ ★ — 3

Ali and His Camera is an interesting book. — 4

I read the book last week and I really liked it. It's not a long book. It's got fifteen pages. There are a lot of great pictures in it.

It's about a boy. His name is Ali. He wants a camera. A woman gives him a camera and he takes photos. Ali meets a man. The man works at a newspaper. I don't want to tell you too much. You should read it for yourself. — 5

Ali and His Camera is a great book and I recommend it to everyone! — 6

Writing Steps

 31 **Write a review of a book or film you liked.**
Use the text in 30 to help you.

1 Think of a book or film.
2 Make a list of what you liked about it.
3 Think of an online name and write today's date.
4 Write a title for your review.
5 Think of how many stars to give the book or film.
6 Write a topic sentence.
7 Write two paragraphs for the body of the review.
8 Write a final sentence.

32 **Listen, read and repeat.**

1 ew   **2** ey   **3** e_e

33 **Listen and find. Then say.**

stew   **grey**   **these**

34 **Listen and blend the sounds.**

1 f-ew   few   **2** h-ey   hey
3 e-ve   eve   **4** n-ew   new
5 p-r-ey   prey   **6** g-e-ne   gene
7 th-ey   they   **8** d-ew   dew

35 **Read aloud. Then listen and chant.**

These three are new!
They eat stew
And wear grey, too!

Values | Learn new things.

36 Listen and look. Find out which activities the people want to try and which they don't.

1

2

3

4

37 Look at 36. Role play with a partner.

Do you know how to build a robot?

No, I don't. But I'd like to learn!

PROJECT

38 Make a Try New Things lottery box.

- **Write activities on cards.**
- **Cut a hole in a box.**
- **Put the cards in the box.**
- **Choose three activities. Pick one to try!**

 tennis

 ice skating

 tap dancing

 bake a pie

 speak French

Write the answers in your notebook.

1 What does she think of making a website? (amazing)

2 What do they think of speaking Chinese? (difficult)

3 What does he think of drawing comic books? (interesting)

4 What do you think of playing badminton? (boring)

 Read and match.

1 **A:** Where are you going tonight?

2 **A:** What do you want?

3 **A:** My knee hurts a lot.

4 **A:** I'm really hot.

a **B:** I think I'll have a pizza, please.

b **B:** I'll get some ice to put on it.

c **B:** Wait, I'll open the window.

d **B:** I think I'll go to the cinema.

 Complete for you. Then ask and answer.

Know how to:

Don't Know how to:

Would like to learn:

What I think about...:

Do you know how to...?

What would you like to learn how to do?

What do you think of...?

I Can

• talk about things people know how to do.

• give opinions and make offers and quick decisions.

• describe how my body moves.

• write a review.

How Well Do I Know It? Can I Use It?

1 Think about it. Read and draw. Practise.

😊 I know this.　　😐 I need more practice.　　☹️ I don't know this.

1	**Special days:** Earth Day, Father's Day, my parents' anniversary, New Year's Day...	**PAGES** 112	😊	😐	☹️
2	**Ways to celebrate:** give/get presents, have a party, watch fireworks...	113	😊	😐	☹️
3	**Hobbies:** basketball, chess, coin collection, doll collection, video games...	128	😊	😐	☹️
4	**Talents:** bake a cake, build a robot, draw comic books, make a website...	144	😊	😐	☹️
5	We're **going to** celebrate tomorrow. **Is** he **going to** give presents? Yes, he **is**./ No, he **isn't**. 1st – first, 10th – tenth, 20th – twentieth...	116–117	😊	😐	☹️
6	Sam **cooked** a lot because he**'s going to** have a party.	120–121	😊	😐	☹️
7	Laura is a **good** chess player. Yoko is a **better** chess player **than** Laura. Alex is **the best** chess player in the class. I'm **more organised than** my Dad. Skydiving is **the most interesting** hobby. I'm **good at/bad at** video games.	132–133, 136–137	😊	😐	☹️
8	**Do** you **know how to play** the piano? She**'d like to learn how to** sing. What **do** they **think of** snowboarding? They **think** it's dangerous.	148–149	😊	😐	☹️
9	**I'll** help you if you're tired. **I'll** have pizza and a cola, please.	152–153	😊	😐	☹️

187

2 **Get ready.**

A Complete the dialogue. Use the correct form of the words in the box and a form of be going to. Then listen and check.

> be (x2)   dance   do (x2)   play   sing   skateboard

Samuel: Hey, ¹❓ you ²❓ something for the school talent show on 9ᵗʰ May?

Melissa: I don't know. Maybe. Who ³❓ in it?

Samuel: Well, Katie and Julia ⁴❓ .

Melissa: Oh, wow! They're better dancers than I am.

Samuel: And Lucas asked for a piano because he ⁵❓ .

Melissa: He's the best singer in the class! What else can I do?

Samuel: Let's see... Ricardo ⁶❓ . He's very good at skateboarding. And Jen ⁷❓ the guitar.

Melissa: Hey, I know what I can do!

Samuel: Great. What?

Melissa: I can catch food. Watch! [*Melissa throws some food and catches it in her mouth.*]

Melissa: ⁸❓ anyone else ⁹❓ that at the talent show?

Samuel: No, I don't think so.

Melissa: Excellent! I ¹⁰❓ the best food catcher at the show!

Samuel: Ha, ha. And the most interesting! Wait, I'll help you practise!

B Practise the dialogue in **A** with a partner.
Then practise again. Make up your own answers.

C Ask and answer the questions with a partner.

1 Why doesn't Melissa want to sing or dance in the talent show?

2 What special talents have you got? Explain.

3 **Get set.**

 STEP 1 Make a poster for a school talent show. First, cut out the strips on page 161 of your Activity Book.

 STEP 2 Glue the strips onto a sheet of paper or poster board.

 STEP 3 Design your poster. Add your own pictures and text. Now you're ready to **Go!**

> I think Leia's poster is the best one. It's got the coolest design!

Talent Show
in the
School Auditorium
Friday, 10ᵗʰ July
7:00 P.M.–8:00 P.M.

4 **Go!**

A Hang up your posters around the classroom. Look at all the posters and vote on the best one.

B Make a sign-up sheet for your poster and hang it on the wall. Go around the class and sign up for five other talent shows. Choose a different talent for each one.

NAME	TALENT
Luisa	sing my favourite song
Celia	dance
Ricky	play the piano

SIGN-UP!

play the piano

C Compare sign-up sheets with your classmates. Work in a group. Tell the group what people are going to do in your talent show.

> Ricky is going to play the piano at the talent show!

5 **Write about yourself in your notebook.**

- What do you usually do at parties?

- What do you do on school holidays?

- What are you going to do at the weekend?

- What hobbies or talents have you got?

- Who's the oldest person in your family? Who's younger than you? Who's the funniest and who's the most organised?

All About Me Date:_____

_____

_____

How Well Do I Know It Now?

6 A **Look at page 160 and your notebook. Draw again.**

B **Use a different colour.**

C **Read and think.**

I can ask my teacher for help.

I can practise.

7 **Rate this Checkpoint.**

 very easy   easy   hard   very hard   fun   OK   not fun

7

8

9

Units 7–9 Exam Preparation

– Part A –

Listen, colour and write. There is one example.

– Part B –

Read the text. Choose the right words and write them on the lines.

Flowers

Example   Most towns _____*have*_____ got a flower shop. These shops sell lots
1   of different flowers all year. You can find _____ in many
2   colours. Some are cheap and others are _____ expensive.
Some people like buying flowers for themselves or for a festival. But
3   they also make very good presents. _____ loves them.

You can buy them in a flower shop, a market and sometimes in
4   a supermarket. If it's someone's birthday, you can _____
flowers. Also if there is a party, guests can take some flowers.
5   People often celebrate _____ anniversaries with flowers –
you give them or receive them.

Example	had	have	has
1	them	it	their
2	most	much	more
3	Nobody	Everyone	Someone
4	give	giving	gives
5	our	theirs	their

Wordlist

Find these words in your language. Then write them in your notebook.

Unit 1	Page	Unit 2	Page	Unit 3	Page
blonde	4	eat out	20	cereal with milk	36
bright	4	go on holiday	20	chicken curry	36
clever	4	go to a wedding	20	lamb meatballs	36
dark	4	go to the dentist	20	noodle soup	36
friendly	4	have a guitar lesson	20	paella	36
funny	4	visit my grandparents	20	porridge	36
glasses	4	cool	21	steamed buns	36
hair	4	every	21	toasted cheese sandwich	36
light	4	once	21	watermelon	36
my	4	three times	21	meal	37
serious	4	twice a year	21	so	37
short	4	weekend	22	sweet	37
shy	4	advertisement	26	lemonade	38
straight	4	attractive	26	sour	39
tall	4	billboard	26	sugar	39
wavy	4	catch your eye	26	balanced	42
chair	5	character	26	dairy	42
curly	5	company	26	diet	42
different	5	jingle	26	fat	42
her	5	popular	26	grains	42
our	5	product	26	protein	42
same	5	remember	26	salty	42
common	6	slogan	26	sugary	42
hers	6	tool	26	wholemeal	42
mine	6	tune	26	filling	46
yours	6	alphabetical order	30	fish cakes	46
nice	7	doorknobs	30	juice box	46
heavy	8	girl	30	prepare	46
ours	9	habits	30	rice	46
their	9	sliding doors	30	meat	47
theirs	9	ice	31	organic	47
your	9	After that	32	pasta	47
birth	10	afternoon	32	risotto	47
exactly	10	Finally	32	because	48
fingerprint	10	Next	32	April	49
fraternal	10	sequence words	32	bubble	49
height	10	bird	33	camel	49
identical	10	curl	33	local	49
pair	10	fur	33	medal	49
quadruplets	10	hurt	33	pupil	49
rare	10	shirt	33	sandals	49
relationship	10	sir	33	towel	49
survive	10	skirt	33	travel	49
triplets	10	surf	33	menu	51
twins	10	turn	33		
dangerous	13				
beard	14				
moustache	14				
year	14				
dear	17				
ear	17				
fair	17				
fear	17				
hear	17				
stairs	17				

Wordlist

Unit 9	Page
bake a cake	144
build a robot	144
draw comic books	144
hip-hop artist	144
make a website	144
new	144
play badminton	144
play the guitar	144
sing like a rock star	144
snowboard	144
speak Chinese	144
bone	150
brain	150
contract	150
flexible	150
joint	150
motion	150
muscle	150
nerves	150
organs	150
precision	150
relax	150
skeleton	150
support	150
system	150
extraordinary	154
genius	154
instrument	154
peaceful	154
professional	154
perform	155
online name	156
rating	156
review	156
dew	157
eve	157
few	157
gene	157
grey	157
hey	157
prey	157
stew	157

Base Form	Simple Past
ask	asked
bake	baked
be	was/were
begin	began
bring	brought
build	built
buy	bought
call	called
catch	caught
celebrate	celebrated
change	changed
come	came
cook	cooked
cut	cut
destroy	destroyed
do	did
draw	drew
drink	drank
drive	drove
eat	ate
explain	explained
fall	fell
feed	fed
feel	felt
fight	fought
find	found
fly	flew
get	got
give	gave
go	went
grow	grew
have	had
hear	heard
help	helped
hit	hit
hold	held
hope	hoped
keep	kept
kill	killed
know	knew
learn	learned
leave	left
like	liked
listen	listened
live	lived
look	looked
lose	lost
love	loved
make	made

Base Form	Simple Past
meet	met
move	moved
need	needed
perform	performed
plan	planned
play	played
put	put
read	read
realize	realized
rest	rested
ride	rode
ring	rang
run	ran
say	said
see	saw
sell	sold
send	sent
sing	sang
sit	sat
skateboard	skateboarded
sleep	slept
snowboard	snowboarded
speak	spoke
stand	stood
start	started
stay up	stayed up
swim	swam
take	took
talk	talked
tell	told
think	thought
throw	threw
travel	travelled
try	tried
turn	turned
understand	understood
use	used
visit	visited
wait	waited
wake up	woke up
walk	walked
want	wanted
wash	washed
watch	watched
wear	wore
worry	worried
write	wrote
yell	yelled

Big English Song

From the mountaintops to the bottom of the sea,
From a big blue whale to a baby bumblebee —
If you're big, if you're small, you can have it all
And you can be anything you want to be!

**It's bigger than you. It's bigger than me.
There's so much to do and there's so much to see!
The world is big and beautiful and so are we!
Think big! Dream big! Big English!**

So in every land, from the desert to the sea
We can all join hands and be one big family.
If we love, if we care, we can go anywhere!
The world belongs to everyone; it's ours to share.

**It's bigger than you. It's bigger than me.
There's so much to do and there's so much to see!
The world is big and beautiful and so are we!
Think big! Dream big! Big English!**

**It's bigger than you. It's bigger than me.
There's so much to do and there's so much to see!
The world is big and beautiful and waiting for me.
A one, two, three...
Think big! Dream big! Big English!**

Pearson Education Limited
Edinburgh Gate
Harlow
Essex CM20 2JE
England
and Associated Companies throughout the world.

www.pearsonelt.com/bigenglish

First published 2015
Twelfth impression 2023
ISBN: 978-1-4479-9447-3

Set in Heinemann Roman
Editorial and design management by hyphen S.A.
Printed and bound by CPI Group (UK) Ltd, Croydon, CR0 4YY

Acknowledgements

The publisher would like to thank the following for their kind permission to
reproduce their photographs:

(Key: b-bottom; c-centre; l-left; r-right; t-top)

123RF.com: akiyoko 126br (kites), Inspirestock International 120tr, Teresa
Kasprzycka 126tr, Lars Kastilan 136tr, Le Moal Olivier 123tl, Andres Rodriguez
18cr/4, Dmitriy Shironosov 34cl/3; **Age Fotostock Spain S.L.:** Imagebroker /
Ulrich Doering 47tl, Patrick G 58tl/1, Martin Mark Soerensen 72c, Jochen Tack
138tl; **Alamy Images:** Idris Ahmed 118tr, Anyka 132cr, H Armstrong Roberts
90br/12, 106br, Jon Berkeley 74tr/3, Alison Bernier 59cr, 106tr, Blend Images
112tl/1, blickwinkel 80tr/d, Anders Blomqvist 112bc/5, Blue Jean Images 35tr,
James Boardman 15t, 15tl, Bon Appetit 43cr, Brand Z 90bc/11, BrazilPhotos.
com 126tc, BSIP SA 66tr, Collection 58tr/4, 73tr, Design Pics Inc 74tl/1, Chuck
Eckert 20tr, Alan Edwards 144cr/6, 159tr, David R. Frazier 144br/10, Raga Jose
Fuste 118cl, Gabbro 148bl, GL Archive 90bl/10, David J. Green - Lifestyle Themes
34tr/2, Jeff Greenberg 144bc/9, 149cl/3, Denise Hager 129c/3, Ernie Janes 134tl,
johnrochaphoto 128cr/6, Kidstock 113tr, Ladi Kirn 113cl, Robert Landau 90tl/1, H
Lefebvre 90bl/7, Justin Leighton 112bl/4, Lordprice Collection 134cr, M Itani 40br,
54bl, MBI 18tl/1, Jeff Morgan 134cl, Michael Newman 129br/4, Nikreates 50br/5
(juice), David Page 20tl, 35tc, Picture Partners 129c/2, Ingolf Pompe 100tl, RGB
Ventures LLC DBA / Superstock 139tl, Pep Roig 96cl, SAGAPhoto.com / Roux
Olivier 144bl/8, Ian Shaw 129bl/1, Joe Sohm 91tr, Stock Illustrations Ltd 14tr,
Peter Stroh 80tl/a, Johan Tack 58c/6, Phil Talbot 97br, The Africa Image Library
74bc/5, Travelshots 79br, 124br, Vintage Images 90br/9, Stacy Walsh Rosenstock
112br/6, Wave Royalty Fee / Design Pics Inc 90tc/5, Wegner P 78b, 83br, Sara
Zinelli 15tr, Zuma Press Inc 142br; **Brand X Pictures:** 18cl/3; **Corbis:** Blend Images
/ Andersen Ross 113c, Blue Jean Images 4bl/2, George D. Lepp 74bl/4, Minden
Pictures / Pete Oxford 81br, Kazuyoshi Nomachi 118br (background), Reuters /
Mick Tsikas 155cl, Ariel Skelley 126tl; **DK Images:** Ian OLeary 74tc/2; **Fotolia.
com:** Alekss 6-7, 18-19, ameli k 128tl/1, anankkml 75tr, Subbotina Anna 29cl/1,
Artranq 90tl/4, AZP Worldwide 29cr/3, Benicce 90tr/3, Jörg Beuge 47tr, Blend
Images 40cr/2, 52tr (Boy), 160tr, Javier Brosch 153tr, burakdemirezen 36cr/6,
Catmando 85bl, Jacek Chabraszewski 25bl, 34bl, 51br, 62bl, 72cl, 81bl, 83cr, 88cl,
95br, 99tr, 104cl, 108bl, 149tl/1, 151cl, chasingmoments 9bl, 21br, 30cl, 51bl, 68c,
81cr, 88cr, 99tl, 120bl, 135cr, 153bc, 158cr, CJPhoto 128tc/2, Andy Dean 37br/4,
DennisNata 58tr/3, Nina Dezhda 36tr, dimedrol68 14c/d, DMM Photography Art
134br, dream79 126br (origami), Pavel Drozda 68tl/b, elen studio 113br, ExQuisine
36bc, Julie Eydman 40bl, Jurgen Falchle 128bl/7, Flowerpower 113bl, 160c/top,
fotodesign-jegg.de 4tr/4, freestyleone 36tl/1, Keith Frith 58br/10, funky_soul
88tc, Gelpi 10bl, goldenangel 145r, 160br, Goldpix 91, Sanjay Goswami 127br, Joe
Gough 36c/2, 36br, Michael Gray 40c, haveseen 74br/6, 86br, Ramona Heim
58tl/2, iofoto 116br (boy), 116br (woman), 126tc (flag), JackF 28tr, Jarp 36c/5, jjpixs
35tl, karelnoppe 4tc/3, Karen & Uwe Annas 16tr, kazakovmaksim 80tc/c, Ivan
Kmit 128tr/3, Valeriy Lebedev 13br, 45br, 62br, 83cl, 95bl, 137cl, 151cr, Konstantin
Li 144cr/7, lilufoto 149cr/4, lucigrumeza 88tr, mattiaath 82tr, monitcellllo 48br,
52bc, Monkey Business 9br, 18bl, 20cr, 25tr, 30cr, 34tl/1, 52tr, 75br, 126cr,
135cl, 142cl, 149br, 154cr, Monkey Business Images 102br, nami66 13bl, 81cl, 104cr,
120cl, 129cr, 137cr, 153bl, 158cl, Anna Omelchenko 18br, 75bl, 89cr, 132br, 142cr,
149bl, 154cl, Pete Pahham 40cl/1, Thomas Perkins 37bl/2, Pink Candy 128c/5,
poonsap 36bl, 40cr, pzRomashka 58cr/7, Radu Razvan 14c/c, rpo7 80tc/b, RT
Images 50br/2 (Fruit), Michael Schutze 29c/5, Uryadnikov Sergey 78t, 78c, 85tl,
siraphol 126br (ricecake), Snow Queen 13tr, sunabesyou 58bl/8, 63br, taka 126br
(costume), Max Topchii 10cl, txakel 13tl, Viktor 50br/4 (chicken), Dani Vincek

44tr, Vitalinko 10tl, Wavebreakmediamicro 156bl, xy 12tr, Alexander Yakovlev
144tl/1, zest_marina 36cl/4, 40bc, 48tr, 50br/6 (Melon); **Getty Images:** Melanie
Acevedo 152tr, Rhienna Cutler 18tr/2, Fuse 4bl/1, 75l, Kidstock 5r, Amos Morgan
5l, Morsa Images / Digital Vision 99br, Katarina Premfors 25br, 126cl, The
Image Bank 14c/a; **Glow Images:** Maskot 58tr, Radius Images 21tr, 52br, Naho
Yoshizawa 46tl; **Imagestate Media:** John Foxx Collection 144tr/4; **Omimages
Photography:** Photographersdirect.com 69tr/c; **Pearson Education Ltd:** Studio
8 98tr, Jon Barlow 58bc/9, 127bc, Gareth Boden 37bc/3, Tudor Photography
46tr; **Reuters:** Str Old 154tr; **Rex Features:** Sinopix 154tl; **Shutterstock.com:** 72c,
Peter Albrektsen 128cl/4, 160cr/btm, Galyna Andrushko 75, Subbotina Anna 43c,
archideaphoto 5b, Andrey Arkusha 14c/b, Artix Studio 46-47, AVAVA 128br/8,
bds 90tc/2, bikerider london 90tr/6, bikeworldtravel 112c, Brandon Blinkenberg
5t, bonchan 119br, 119br (churros), BortN 59t, Franck Boston 37bl/1, Cheryl Casey
129cr, Sam Chadwick 96tr, Chatchawan 74-75b, ciarada 144-145 (background),
CLS Design 52cr, Denizo71 34cr/4, dpaint 112-113 (background), 122-123
(background), Andrey Eremin 58, fusebulb 64cr (bacteria), Warren Goldswain
144tc/2, Rob Hainer 29cr/6, Chris Harvey 139tr, Horiyan 50br/3 (milk), Charlie
Hutton 9cl, 96br, Innershadows Photography 144c/3, 148bc, irin-k 74, Jezper 10l,
11r, Kalim 68tl/a, 106cr, Sebastian Kaulitzki 64cr (virus), Malgorzata Kistryn 47c,
Lukasz Kurbiel 79c, Ru Bai Le 74-75, Lebendkulturen.de 64tr (protozoa), Lepas
69br, Marmion 37br/5, Monkey Business Images 29c/2, 32tr, Juriah Mosin 140br,
naluwan 148br, 162tr, Luba V Nel 47t, nikkytok 64br (fungi), Nils Z 43bc, Sura
Nualpradid 58-59, Donskaya Olga 4br/6, Dennis Radovanovic 149tr/2, Joshua
Resnick 44cr, shama 106cr (tiger), strelka 69tr/d, studio online 50br/a (salad),
sunsetman 88tl, Bayanova Svetlana 90b, topten22photo 118bl, Triff 29cl/4,
Kiselev Andrey Valerevich 4bc, Evlakhov Valeriy 36-37, Peter Weber 144cl/5, Tracy
Whiteside 127bl, wormdog 62, YorkBerlin 150r, Yurchyks 72bc, Zhukov 64-65;
SuperStock: 20cl, Asia Images 20bl, Blend Images 112cl/2, Burger / Phanie 91cl,
Denkou Images 37tr, Glow Images 90bc/8, Lisette Le Bon 113cr, Stockbroker /
Purestock 20br

Cover images: *Front:* **Shutterstock.com:** Lukasz Kurbiel c, Rudchenko Liliia l;
SuperStock: Corbis r

All other images © Pearson Education

Illustrated by
Sean@KJA-Artists, Matt Latchford, Victor Moshopoulos, Zaharias Papadopoulos
(hyphen), Jamie Pouge, Christos Skaltsas (hyphen)